THE PANCAKE MEMOS

THE PANCAKE MEMOS

AND OTHER STORIES FOR GROWING CHRISTIANS

Tales of drama, humor, and allegory
about following Christ
in daily, down-to-earth style

BY ED STEWART

Beacon Hill Press of Kansas City
Kansas City, Missouri

ISBN: 083-411-3880

Printed in the
United States of America

Cover Design: Crandall Vail

10 9 8 7 6 5 4 3 2 1

This collection of short stories
is dedicated with love
to my mother-in-law, Ann Wilson.

CONTENTS

"Pursued by Love," "Money to Burn," "Corridors," "Adam Waits," and "The Mesori" were originally published in separate issues of *Sunday Digest.*

1

CITY-BY-THE-DUNES

AARON CRACKED HIS GAVEL three times on a large, flat rock. "The monthly meeting of the board of directors will now come to order," he chanted mechanically. The vice-chairman continued rapping on the rock until the 12 board members, sitting cross-legged before him on the woven straw mat, finally quieted. Only the flaps of the conference tent, teased by the warm desert breeze, chattered on disrespectfully.

"The tribe of Benjamin has the honor of delivering the invocation this morning," Aaron monotoned dryly. "Abidan, prince of the Benjamites, please lead us."

Abidan rose ceremoniously from his place at the back of the tent and strode forward, hands clasped piously below his scraggly beard. Upon reaching Aaron's side at the front, he turned to face his peers, spread his hands condescendingly over the small congregation and, in well-practiced angelic tenor, quavered, "Let us pray."

As the remaining board members dutifully wrinkled their faces into masks of reverence, Abidan intoned a long and lavishly detailed invocation. Seizing his moment of glory, the young Benjamite thee'd and thou'd his way through the wonders of Israel's deliverance from Egypt, proudly extolling his tribe for its faithfulness in obeying the

Decalogue. After countless minutes, Abidan's melodramatic, singsongy tone had lulled most of the board members into a stupor. Heads were beginning to drop to the mat like spoiled figs from a tree.

But Elizur the Reubenite, sitting in the front row, was wide awake and steaming with impatience. Finally he grabbed the hem of Abidan's skirt and gave an impatient jerk. Without skipping a syllable, the junior board member took the cue and obediently nosedived toward an eloquent conclusion, including a petition for God's blessing on the golf tournament following the meeting.

By the time Abidan had warbled the last of seven amens, all the board members were again sitting piously erect—except for the chairman of the board.

Moses sat cross-legged on the mat to Aaron's left, bent forward at the waist. His face, hovering a few inches above the mat, was buried in his massive, leathered hands. Everyone could hear Moses' subdued but earnest prayer above the *whish* of the wind-whipped sand spraying the outside of the tent.

The board members rolled their eyes at each other knowingly as their leader prayed on, oblivious to Abidan's conclusion. Sentimental old codger, they thought. Losing your grip on reality, are you? Retreating to the good old days of the burning bush? A few of the men flirted with slumber again while others, including Aaron, just stared at the chairman, who was so adept at prolonging a one-hour board meeting into a two-hour ordeal with his penchant for prayer.

Presently, Elizur, wringing his hands with urgency, startled his peers by clearing his throat loudly. Aaron scowled at him and raised a finger to his lips to motion silence. But it was too late. Moses rubbed the tears from his eyes, wiped his hands on his skirt, and sat up.

His bloodshot eyes scanned the board members seated before him, then narrowed slightly as he eyed Elizur. What's on your agenda that's so all-fired important? Moses' perceptive squint inquired. Elizur bowed to avert the prickly stare and pretended that he didn't hear the chairman's silent question. You'll know soon enough, old man, the Reubenite mouthed to himself.

Aaron and the other board members, who had heard every unspoken word between Moses and Elizur, anxiously awaited the chairman's signal to get on with the meeting. Moses again surveyed the men before him. "Amen," he said at last.

"Amen," the board members breathed with relief.

The minutes were read and received without comment, as were the financial statements and several perfunctory committee reports. Several items of old business were efficiently dispatched, prompted by Elizur the Reubenite who cut short each discussion with an anxious call for the question.

Elizur's push through the agenda was not totally foreign to the board members. As the board's most avid golfer, Elizur was the champion of early adjournment to the monthly tournament in the Sinai foothills. But today Elizur seemed to have more on his mind than his handicap.

"The first item of new business concerns a proposal by Elizur, the prince of the tribe of Reuben." Aaron nodded toward the Reubenite. "Brother Elizur now has the floor."

The Reubenite stood quickly. "Gentlemen," he began while shuffling a sheaf of notes, "I'll make this brief."

"So you can have some extra time on the driving range with your new Egyptian woods?" an anonymous voice poked from the rear of the group. A burst of laughter shook the tent.

Elizur smiled nervously as he glanced at a deadpanned Moses. "I wish to bring before the board a matter that came up at the Reubenite steering committee meeting almost two months ago. It concerns our 12-month stay in the Sinai and our alleged destination."

"*Alleged* destination?" whispered several board members simultaneously, incredulity wrinkling their brows.

"Now, gentlemen," Elizur's voice rose above the murmuring, "please hear me out." The whispering subsided and Elizur, noticing that Moses was leaning slightly toward him, began again.

"As you know, God graciously responded to our plight in Egypt and activated our release through his esteemed servant Moses. Praise the Lord!"

"Praise the Lord!" echoed the brethren routinely. Every member knew well the strategy of hyping the board with a recitation of Israel's miraculous recent history.

"And God in His mercy led us out of our captivity, annihilated our captors, and brought us to Sinai, the mountain of His presence. Praise the Lord!"

"Praise the Lord!" the men chanted. Elizur glanced at Moses in time to see him chime in. At least he likes it so far, the prince of Reuben mused cautiously.

"We have been blessed with the spoils of our Egyptian overlords and . . ."

"Elizur, if you please!" interrupted an irritated Aaron. "We have other business and time is running short. Will you get to the point!"

Moses' eyes were riveted on Elizur's perspiring face. "Yes," the chairman said, uncharacteristically attentive to the proceedings. "The point, Elizur."

The tent was a vacuum of silence. Eyes flitted between Elizur and Moses. The growing tension even seemed to stifle the late morning breeze. The flaps fell silent.

"The point is," Elizur surprised himself with the force of his own voice, "where do we think we're going? That cloud out there hasn't budged in a year. We've been telling ourselves that we are destined for a so-called Promised Land none of us has ever seen. All the while we've been sitting in the very shadow of God's presence."

Elizur quickly stooped to retrieve a large scroll from the mat where he had been sitting. "Therefore," his voice squawked nervously as he approached his point, "the tribe of Reuben hereby proposes the founding of City-by-the-

Dunes, a permanent metropolis for the people of God!" When the Reubenite prince shouted "permanent" he unfurled a huge papyrus blueprint detailing a massive planned community that made Pithom and Raameses look like shantytowns.

After all the breathable air had been sucked from the tent in deep gasps of surprise, the board members began exhaling their retorts:

"Incredible!"

"Unbelievable!"

"Why didn't we think of this before?"

"We have the manpower to sink irrigation wells all over the desert floor!"

"We can grow vegetables and fruits!"

"No more manna! No more quail!"

"Praise the Lord! Praise the Lord! Praise the . . ."

No one could remember the last time Moses had stood to address the board. Overspiritual, semisenile figureheads were to be seen, not heard. But suddenly there he was, with his staff in hand, hovering over the delegation.

"Sit down!" Moses barked angrily at the prince of Reuben as he swung his staff in Elizur's direction. The bug-eyed prince dived to the mat just as the staff whistled through the air precisely where his head had been a split second earlier. The tent was again breathlessly silent.

"Enough!" Moses cried, louder than anyone had heard him cry since the day he smashed the first set of tablets. "I've had enough of your blithering about what *you* think!"

Moses' tunic rippled around his trembling frame, and his knuckles blanched while strangling his staff as if it were an asp.

"Jehovah ripped you from the grasp of the Egyptians at the cost of countless thousands of Egyptian sons and Israeli lambs. But before your sandals had cooled from the exodus, *you* thought it would be nice to have a golden calf to thank!"

The deliverer's eyes blazed as hot as his words, and the

board members cowered as if sitting too close to an over-stoked furnace.

"Jehovah gave you bread you did not bake and quail you did not breed, and plenty of it to enjoy in the leisure of your liberty. But with the crumbs still in your beards and the meat between your teeth, *you* thought, Wouldn't it be wonderful to chomp into an Egyptian onion again back at the Pharaoh's brickworks."

Moses strode heavily through the tent jamming his staff through the straw floor mat with every exclamation.

"And now, after God has painstakingly organized you and unified you to return to the land that has your name written all over it, *you* think this cozy little wasteland in the Egyptian suburbs will be a swell place to settle down, raise grandchildren, and play golf!" Again Moses slashed his staff through the air, grazing the turban of one of tallest board members.

Then the chairman paused, trying to calm himself. Slowly the red drained from his face. "Whatever happened to good, old-fashioned obedience?" His voice was suddenly controlled and tinged with melancholy. "I was content back in Midian, enjoying a comfortable life herding sheep and raising a family." The weathered leader allowed the hint of a smile to relax the anger on his face. The quivering board members silently released the collective breath they had been holding for several moments.

"But the God of the burning bush blasted me out of my complacent sandals one day," Moses was deadly serious again, "and He said, 'Moses, I have a rescue job for you.' When I heard His plan, I didn't think I could do it, and I surely didn't want to do it. But He was rather convincing when He said, 'If you want any part of Me, you will do what I say.'

"So I accepted this thankless job of leading you out of Egypt. And apparently about 3 million of you agreed that obeying God at that point was a good idea because you followed me out."

After a lip-licking, eye-twitching silence, Moses began to pace again. "Then somebody had the bright idea that God needed our help." The chairman's anger began to simmer and return the color to his face. "So you stopped calling yourselves the board of *elders* and became the board of *directors.* You did less praying and serving in order to do more decision making." Moses' voice began to rumble like a volcano signaling an imminent eruption. His staff stabbed the mat repeatedly, and the board members quickly pulled their toes underneath their skirts.

Then Moses screamed, bulging the veins on his temples and neck. "And now we want to vote on changing God's mind about the location of the Promised Land!" His strained voice turned to a screechy, sarcastic whine. "We don't like living in tents. We want security. We want comfort. We want a country club." The board members shuddered as they watched their leader discard the last shred of control and explode. "Balderdash!"

Moses tried to clear his voice but could only muster a strained whisper. "Well-I-have-a-mo-tion-for-you-board-of-di-rec-tors!" The chairman jabbed his staff toward Aaron and each of the board members with each crisply enunciated syllable. "Since obedience to God got us this far, I move that we continue to obey God. I move that if God says, 'Build a city,' we build a city. But I move that if God says, 'Be ready to travel at a moment's notice,' we stay ready to travel."

Suddenly the fire in Moses' eyes crystallized into two icy hot arrows that he aimed at the mouths-agape board members. His next raspy proclamation was more spat than spoken. "And I further move that if God says, 'Execute the board of elders for insubordination,' we execute the board of elders." The chairman swept his staff upward like an executioner's sword, then jerked it fiercely down to where Aaron's gavel lay, smashing it to splinters with an ear-popping crack. Several of the board members lurched and yelped at the sound. Elizur fainted dead away with a sickly moan.

Finally Moses straightened himself indignantly. "All in favor of obeying God," he whispered, "say, 'Aye.'" The words had barely passed his lips when the air was split by a horrendous crash that concaved the tent walls, bowed its poles, and sent the already terrified board members screaming into each other's arms.

"The cloud!" a young boy shrieked as he burst into the tent and dived to his knees in front of Moses. "My lord," the boy panted hysterically, "the cloud is moving!"

Four hours later only a few telltale remnants identified the sprawling desert beneath smoldering Sinai as the former campsite of the Israeli population. On the crest of a dune lay a half-buried straw mat riddled with punctures and strewn with olive wood splinters. Near the foothills someone had carelessly abandoned a nice, new set of Egyptian woods. And high on the mountain's slope, driven by a fierce wind and pinwheeling dangerously close to the fiery summit, flapped a tattered papyrus blueprint.

FOR THOUGHT AND DISCUSSION

1. This fictitious story is loosely based on Num. 9:15-23. What elements, as represented in the behavior of the board of directors, had wrongly replaced obedience to God?
2. Read Acts 5:27-29. What instruction did the apostles disobey in order to maintain obedience to God?
3. Under what circumstances today, if any, is it appropriate for Christians to disobey civil authorities in order to maintain obedience to God?
4. When do you find it most difficult to maintain obedience to God?

2

REENTRY

David McClain tried to ignore the insistent *ping* coming from the Oldsmobile's engine compartment. Another tank of bad gas, he hoped silently, pushing away nagging suspicions of car trouble. David's downtown Los Angeles office and its hassles were already several miles behind him. All he really wanted to think about for the next two hours was the beautiful young woman from his office waiting for him in Palm Springs and how much fun they would steal from the weekend manager's conference. No bugs, no glitches, please, he begged any gods who might be listening.

"Oh, no!" David groaned aloud, then breathed a bitter curse. His eyes fastened on the rearview mirror and the angry clouds of smoke billowing menacingly from behind the car. He flipped on his right turn signal and watched for a break in the roaring river of Friday afternoon traffic escaping the city. A few sympathetic motorists slowed allowing the disabled Olds to ease across three lanes to the paved shoulder.

Once the car had stopped David detected a hissing sound and the odor of steam and hot rubber. It's not smoke, it's steam, he assured himself with guarded relief. Must be something wrong with the radiator. The ping must be from the engine overheating. He muttered another expletive, underscoring his disgust that his heavenly weekend was being delayed by such an earthy obstruction.

David McClain, a trim and tanned executive in his early 30s, had ascended the Dynar Systems ladder as easily as a rocket, guided by one of his company's computers, reached the heavens. Beginning in sales, David steadily scaled the marketing division to the rung of director in less than six years. With every new title came increasing measures of intangible yet gratifying prestige and tangible salary hikes. These commodities served David well in obtaining the status-enriching trophies for which he hungered. He had his corner office, his diamond jewelry, his luxury Oldsmobile, and his athletic club membership. And waiting for him in Palm Springs was the sweetest prize—Valerie, Dynar's alluringly available production assistant.

David often thought of his meteoric rise in terms of a successful launch into space—a feat that epitomized Dynar's success in the industry. The grueling, competitive pressures that scraped his insides raw were like the G forces pounding the astronauts as they were propelled into orbit. The trip to the top was painful, even scary at times, making every cell of the body scream, "Slow down!" But at the same time the trip was ecstatically thrilling. "What a ride!" David enjoyed quipping in the midst of a pressure-filled project at the office.

During his ascent David had unceremonially jettisoned some stages of his past as if they were spent fuel cells. Two years earlier he left behind a wife who bored him nightly with earthbound trivia: menus, wallpaper designs, kitchenware parties, and names for a son they never conceived. Subsequent to the divorce David abandoned vestiges of sexual morality from his arid religious upbringing. Several brief experimental relationships bridged the painful gap between his marriage and his fascination with Valerie, the playgirl of the L.A. office.

Other values of his past that had not yet been discarded

were poised for imminent separation. His idealistic honesty was being seduced and spoiled by the temptation to skulduggery so often infecting those competing for high-tech megabucks. "Stab anyone who stands in the way of a successful sale," was the office code of conduct. Furthermore, David's lifelong commitment to moderation in his vices was being consumed in the flames of his streaking success. His harmless after-dinner drink was now preceded by two or three beers on the way home from the office, a two-martini lunch, and sometimes a screwdriver with his eggs benedict. He wasn't above any substance or experience that might keep him in the right crowd or the right frame of mind for soaring in his chosen field.

David McClain realized that he was no longer a shooting star, however. He was established, he had arrived, he was in orbit. He was more like an orbiting sun—though perhaps a minor one—in a galaxy of information age luminaries. But in his quieter moments David was plagued by an unsettled, nameless feeling somewhat akin to the weightlessness the astronauts talked about. Having found a place in the high-tech solar system, David sometimes felt detached or untethered, like being lost in space with no hope of rescue or return to earth. He had assumed that the ecstasy of the ride and the fulfillment of his arrival would fill his gnawing inner void. But in his rare moments of solitude, David yearned for something solid under his feet again.

When he lifted the hood of the car, David was momentarily engulfed by a cloud of steam bursting from the engine compartment. He was about to retreat to his car phone to dial the auto club when an old Datsun station wagon braked abruptly in the slow lane and swerved onto the shoulder in front of the Olds. A man climbed out of the Datsun and jogged back to where David stood. He was tall and wiry thin. He wore rumpled brown slacks and a brownish plaid, grease-stained shirt that looked like it had been used for a shop rag.

"Having some car trouble?" the man inquired cordially.

"Yeah, I guess I'm overheated," David returned a forced smile that mirrored his uneasiness at facing the stranger.

The man leaned under the hood where the clouds of steam were diminishing to swirling puffs. "Looks like one of your heater hoses is cracked," the man called out while bobbing his head over the engine. "I have all the tools and parts in my car needed to change that hose. I'll be happy to do it for you. It shouldn't take more than 20 minutes."

David wondered if the stranger really knew how to replace the hose correctly and how much he would overcharge him for emergency roadside service. The man was at least 50, David estimated, with thinning brown and gray hair. The man's shabby clothing belied the air of professionalism that David detected in his demeanor. He's not your ordinary roadside panhandler, David calculated.

"Are you some kind of roving mechanic?" David asked, buying more time for his evaluation.

"Yes, in a way," the man's smile broadened. "I've been unemployed for several months, so I spend a lot of time on the freeway lending a hand where I can."

David finally acquiesced, convinced that the man could get him on the road to Palm Springs faster than the auto club: "I'd appreciate any help you could give." Then he stuck out a tentative hand. "My name is David McClain."

"My friends call me Mack," the man returned, accepting David's hand. "I'll have you rolling in just a few minutes."

Mack retrieved some tools from the Datsun and began cautiously removing the damaged hose. David stood awkwardly by the fender watching.

"What kind of work are you looking for?" David hoped to keep the man's price down by making friendly conversation.

"My background is in electronics," Mack almost grunted the words as he struggled to pull the old hose from its fittings. "Actually, computers are my main interest."

"Oh, really!" David brightened at the mention of his

own field. "What branch of the business? Programming? Analysis?"

"I've done a little bit of everything," Mack said as he continued pulling at the damaged hose. "But most of my time has been spent in hardware design and production."

David was pleased that his hunch about Mack's professionalism was correct. "Who have you worked for?" he asked eagerly.

"I started with Tech-point." Mack reappeared from under the hood holding the old hose triumphantly. "But I spent most of my career with Emgraph in Santa Clara."

"Emgraph," David's voice rose with surprise. "Very impressive. They've put together some outstanding instruments for such a small organization." Mack flashed a knowing smile. Then he retreated to the Datsun and returned with a length of hose that matched the one he had removed.

David proudly explained his connection with Dynar, then turned the conversation back to Mack's former employer. "Whatever happened to old man Mills, the big kahuna at Emgraph? I heard he ended up at the bottom of a bottle and his board squeezed him out."

Mack was silent until he finished tightening the screws on the hose clamp. "Yep," he said as he twisted the second clamp into place. "Old man Mills had some problems all right, but he seems to be doing better these days."

"You know Mills personally?" David exclaimed excitedly.

Again Mack said nothing until he had screwed down the second clamp. Then he unfolded from under the hood and faced David, wiping perspiration mixed with condensed steam from his forehead with the back of his hand. "I *am* old man Mills."

Instantly Mack's facial features jibed with David's sketchy memory of a photograph of Eugene Macklin Mills, founder and past president of Emgraph Incorporated. The young executive swallowed a gasp of surprise.

E. M. Mills became a legend in the data processing industry while David was still earning his M.B.A. Indeed, young McClain and his colleagues feasted on case studies of Mills' success. As a "comer" with Tech-point, Mills boldly broke away to form Emgraph on a shoestring. The fledgling hardware design plant launched a line of innovative commercial hardware that rocked the industry. But shortly after Emgraph was ensconced in the Silicon Valley, Mills mysteriously dropped from public view. During the years of David's ascendancy with Dynar, Emgraph remained a formidable competitor, but Eugene Macklin Mills was no more than a name embossed on the company's letterhead.

David was so shocked at Mack's personal revelation that his next question tumbled from his mouth automatically: "How in the world did you get from Emgraph to running a repair service on the San Bernardino Freeway?"

"It really does sound crazy, doesn't it?" Mack chuckled at the ludicrous contrast. "It's a long story, Mr. McClain, and I don't want to keep you from your trip." Mack motioned toward the suit bag hanging in the backseat.

Again David's words leaped into his mouth. "Mr. Mills, we idolized you at Stanford, and I have dreamed of duplicating your success. You and Emgraph hit the moon, sir! And now you're a grease-stained, happy-go-lucky freeway fix-it man. You have left behind everything I am still breeding ulcers to achieve." David's eyes suddenly reflected desperation. "Sir, I *must* hear your story."

Mack smiled and nodded, then announced that his fee for services rendered was a hamburger and a glass of iced tea. Within 20 minutes the two men were huddled around a table in a freeway-side restaurant with iced tea in front of them and burgers on the grill.

"As you already know," Mack began, "everything we touched at Emgraph turned to gold. And as the esteemed guru of the outfit, I caught most of the bouquets—and loved every minute of it. There were lectures, conferences, parties —and endless rounds of cocktails and adoring females eager to slip their hotel keys into my coat pocket. Before long the sweet smell of success consisted mainly of the aroma of Scotch mixed with the exotic fragrances worn by my female associates."

Mack paused to poke at the ice cubes in his tea. David was uncomfortably aware that Mills' story was not matching the glittering case studies he read as a business student. He also sensed that Mack was experiencing some discomfort from his journey into the past.

"I watched lots of guys drown in the sauce and the ladies, and I always bragged, 'It'll never happen to me,'" Mack pressed on determinedly. "But I started drinking earlier in the day and staying out later at night with my girlfriends. My wife saw the handwriting on the wall and bailed out.

"The divorce slowed me down for a while, but soon I was out of control again—drinking heavily, partying, spending hundreds of dollars each month entertaining my groupies. I started tapping into my expense account to fund my life-style, and that's when the board cut me off. About two years ago they 'promoted' me to president emeritus, granted me a generous monthly stipend, and shoved me out the door."

David swallowed dryly, feeling an inner pain from his hero's humiliation. Mack's eyes became slightly moist, so David respectfully occupied himself with a sip of tea.

"Looking back, I can honestly say that the board's action was the best thing that could have happened to me," Mack continued, and David leaned closer with interest. "You see, at Emgraph I really *had* reached the moon. I had everything and everyone I wanted. But when I looked around, there was nobody there but big-time, big-money, big-mouth Mills. And a man with an ego larger than a Saturn rocket is lousy company—even for himself. Like they say, I was lonely in the crowd, alone at the top. No wonder I crammed my life with so many diversions."

It's that weightlessness, that unexplainable feeling of

being lost! David's mind was racing. Mills had been there too!

"Getting booted from Emgraph was like getting kicked off my own private planet and crashing back to Earth in flames," Mack was speaking slower and quieter. "Everything I had lived for was gone. From my vantage point, the crater of my reentry crash was my own grave.

"Since life had already ended for me, suicide was a mere formality. But you know," Mack chuckled at the thought, "I couldn't even do *that* right. I drove my Mercedes off a mountain road at high speed in a drunken stupor one night. The car careened down the mountain, sideswiping trees and boulders, and I bounced around inside like a Ping-Pong ball.

"I woke up in a hospital bed with a little old lady named Florence hovering over me. She said she had seen my car go over the cliff from her cabin and had called the police. She rode with me in the ambulance and sat by my bedside the rest of the night praying for me."

"You'd never seen her before?" David was entranced.

"Never. And she didn't know anything about me either," Mack raised his hand as if swearing the truth. "'It's a miracle o' God that you ain't dead, Mister,' she kept saying."

"On my second day in the hospital Florence told me she was going to read me something from the Bible. I protested a little, saying I wasn't a religious person. But she kindly told me to shut up and listen to the verses God had told her to read to me.

"She proceeded to read several lines that I don't remember. It sounded like jumbled up religious jargon that didn't make sense. But then she read five words that almost knocked me out of my bed: 'You must be born again.' She said Jesus spoke those words to a successful man who felt empty inside. 'It ain't enough to get born once,' she was shaking her finger in my face when she said it. 'You gotta get born again on the inside.'"

Born again? David whined silently. The words had been

uncomfortably lodged in his subconscious since childhood when they were shouted into him by stern-faced statues of piety in a church that seemed estranged from real life. But the words "born again" seemed warm and winsome coming from the lips of E. M. Mills.

"Then Florence asked me if I had been born again," the sparkle was returning to Mack's eyes. "I told her I had already screwed up one life, and I doubted that God wanted to trust me with another. But she insisted that Jesus would put my life together from the inside out if I asked Him to. She said He would make me a brand-new person—like being born all over again." Mack paused while a childlike grin wreathed his weathered face. David had never seen such a smile of contentment on the face of a management level executive. "So I did it," Mack concluded with an affirmative nod.

"Did what?" David snapped frantically as if someone had withheld the final piece from a jigsaw puzzle he was trying to complete.

"I was born again—saved, converted, whatever you want to call it—right there in my hospital room," Mack replied, the grin still brightening his face. "I simply asked Jesus Christ to come into my life and make me brand-new like the Bible said He would. Florence led me in a simple prayer. Then she almost got herself kicked out of the hospital for dancing around my room singing, 'There's a New Name Written Down in Glory,' at the top of her lungs." Mack couldn't help laughing out loud at the description.

But David's expression was more serious. He was hearing the replay of Mack's reentry from his own lonely perch in orbit. He had expected Eugene Macklin Mills to be soaring past the outer galaxies of the business world by now. Instead he had crashed to earth and was more content, composed, and at peace with himself than any high-tech exec David had ever known. "I can't believe that a little old lady evangelist led the founder of Emgraph down the sawdust trail," David's frustration with his own plight was voiced as defensive skepticism of Mack's experience.

"It wasn't just Florence," Mack responded. "It was God using a little old lady as the midwife to my new birth. And believe me, David," Mack leaned across the table to emphasize his point, "Jesus *did* make something new out of me. Before that day I was gagging on my own ego and everything it had accumulated. But now I'm content with a simple life of helping people in trouble and telling my story whenever God presents an opportunity."

Even though he had just met the man, David realized Mack's claim to be different was indisputable. David knew several men in the industry who had soared to prominence, and none of them displayed the humility and contentment Mack exuded. This guy is actually happy about fixing cars for stranded motorists instead of ruling the world of high tech! David exclaimed to himself.

"You mean everybody who is born again turns into a circuit-riding freeway missionary?" David's serious question was veiled with sarcasm.

"No, David," Mack answered. "Christians are different in description and function just like people in all areas of life. For the time being God has given me the assignment of being a 'freeway missionary,' but that may change. Everyone who is born again develops into the unique, fulfilled individual God designed him to be."

The arrival of their hamburgers temporarily dulled the point of the conversation between the two men. David asked a stream of questions about Mack's life over the past two years. Mills had moved to Southern California shortly after his rebirth to live with a sister who was also a Christian. He began attending a small church and devoting much of his time to studying the Bible with its members. He still received a sizable sum from Emgraph each month, but he lived on only a small part of it while using the rest to help people in need.

Yes, Mack hoped to reenter the computer industry some

day—"If the Lord wills," he qualified. "As you know, there are many people in high-tech who are flaming out at the top because all the prizes don't fill the basic emptiness of their lives. If God can use me to direct others in the industry to Him, I'm willing."

David glanced at his watch and realized that he was going to be late for the first meeting of the conference. He suddenly felt very alone, like an astronaut abandoned in space by a crew that had returned to earth without him. He wanted desperately to be back on solid ground where Mack was. And he feared that if he and Mack parted company he would never find his way home.

"David, you're a lucky man," Mack interrupted the younger man's thoughts. At David's expression of disbelief he continued, "You don't have to plunge spinning and burning to the bottom like I did. You can be born again without a painful crash. Why don't you let Jesus start rebuilding your life right now?"

David's heart pounded, and his blood roared in his ears. Mack had suddenly slammed him against the wall with a life-and-death ultimatum. David's competitive spirit challenged him to resist. But the persistent warmth of the humble reborn man staring at him was melting his stubborn resolve.

David was silent until he paid the bill and the two men stepped outside. The sky was dark enough for David to see a few of the brightest stars struggling to shed their light. He thought he saw the glimmer of a satellite coursing through the early evening sky, and another stab of loneliness provoked a silent sigh.

If he had evaluated his next words more carefully he might have rationalized himself into not saying them, but somehow the loneliness he felt formed the sentence and a sudden sense of urgency pushed it out: "Will you help me to be born again, Mr. Mills?" Retrorockets ignited within him. David McClain had aborted orbit and begun his reentry.

FOR THOUGHT AND DISCUSSION

1. How was David's life and career path similar to Mack's? How was it dissimilar?
2. Read John 3:1-8. Based on Jesus' comments to Nicodemus, what does it mean to be born again?
3. If you are a Christian, who was the "Mack" in your life—the most significant person encouraging you toward spiritual birth? For whom are you presently serving as a "Mack"?
4. If you are not a Christian, what needs to happen in your life to move you to a point of spiritual birth?

3

THE MESORI

"MASTER ELIAB! ARE YOU INSIDE?" The voice was that of a Greek with an eastern accent.

Eliab had been napping, but the prospect of a customer opened the innkeeper's eyes. He sat up with a grunt.

"Just a moment!" Eliab called gruffly in Greek. The old man stood with another grunt, straightened his tunic, and waddled outside.

Just inside the courtyard gate stood a fair-skinned man in his early 20s, robed in the colorfully ornamented cloak of eastern nobility. A foreigner with money, the innkeeper hummed to himself eagerly. A majestic horse stood tied to the gate.

"Master Eliab?" The young man bowed courteously, and Eliab affirmed his address with a nod from the doorway. "I am your servant, Bir-Abi, aide to the esteemed Magus Kavir-Meshed from Ecbatana in Media. My master and his fellow travelers await outside your city until I bring them assurance of lodging and some information about an event your townspeople call the Shepherds' Vision."

Eliab sighed quietly. It had been almost a year since anyone in Bethlehem had mentioned the Vision, and even longer since a visitor from Jerusalem or beyond had inquired about the cave or the Child born 20 months ago.

Those had been prosperous days, Eliab reminisced. Scores of Davidites had poured into Bethlehem to register, crowding Eliab's inn and swelling his purse with gold and silver. And then in the midst of census week, the Vision. Shepherds raced wildly through the streets at midnight shouting about a "great light" blazing across the Judean pastureland and an angelic announcement concerning the birth of the Anointed One.

Even more unbelievable, the shepherds were told the exact birthplace of this supposed Messiah—Eliab's stable, a cave carved into the gray limestone hillside behind the inn.

The Vision had caused a great stir in the community, but its credibility was doubted by the respectable Bethlehem citizens. After all, why did the Vision appear to ignorant shepherds instead of the local priests?

Eliab excused the Shepherds' Vision as a hoax or a hallucination. But deep inside him a flicker of wonder stubbornly sparkled in spite of his suffocating logic. Each shepherd's account of the Vision had corroborated the others' testimony to the finest detail. Unusual for a hoax or a dream to be so precise. Secretly, the innkeeper had hoped that the Vision was true.

In the days following the Vision, Eliab had exacted a small toll from the curious onlookers visiting the young family in his stable. When the couple took residence in a small house near the town's edge, Eliab increased his charge and offered patrons a tour inside the cave and an opportunity to touch the trough crib.

But as the ensuing weeks pushed the Vision into the past, the event dimmed in importance to the local residents. Visitors stopped paying to see Eliab's cave. The Child and His parents had blended quietly into Bethlehem's peasant life-style.

"Master Eliab?" The young foreigner punctured the innkeeper's reverie. Eliab was conscious of the opportunity before him.

"Your master is . . . ," he began in Aramaic, caught himself, then began again in Greek. "Your master is welcome in this humble inn, and his servant Eliab will answer all his questions for a small purse of coins." The young man bowed his thanks, mounted his horse, and rode off.

Eliab and his sons had scarcely finished their preparations when the clatter of exuberant voices and the jingle of camel bells from the street announced the arrival of guests. Eliab gasped at the sight. Ten camels. No, 12! And horses, a dozen or more, laden with boxes and satchels. How many men? Many of them servants, but clearly five of them robed in the colorful silk and linen garments of Median magi.

The servants knelt the camels as the five dignitaries dismounted. Bir-Abi, carrying a small black satchel stuffed with gold coins, stepped toward Eliab, who backed into the courtyard in awe. "My master, the Magus Kavir-Meshed of Ecbatana, is hopeful that his gift will adequately comfort his host," the aide offered. Eliab received the satchel with a grin of obvious pleasure. Bir-Abi continued with the formal introductions, and Eliab bowed as low as his portly frame would allow and ushered his guests into the house.

When the five visitors were comfortably reclined on his couch, Eliab opened his mouth to rehearse the Shepherds' Vision. But Kavir-Meshed spoke first. His Greek was flawless and his accent almost imperceptible.

"Our arrival in Judea this week is the culmination of a journey that began in Ecbatana 20 months ago. As you may know, Master Eliab, we serve the Median kings as priests, counselors, and seekers of truth. One morning as we contemplated the predawn heavens, a brilliant mesori flashed into being before our eyes low in the western canopy."

"Mesori?" Eliab leaned toward the magus.

"Mesori is the Egyptian name for a star that is sent to announce the birth of a great prince," Kavir-Meshed responded. "But this mesori was different! It appeared in a formation of stars we call the Shepherd's Staff. The radiant mesori was set in the crook of the staff, transforming it into a magnificently jeweled scepter. And the point of the scepter was aimed precisely at Judea!"

Eliab's heart began to race. The brilliant mesori matches the "great light" of the Shepherds' Vision, he thought breathlessly. The birth of the prince matches the birth of the Anointed One. The story of the Shepherds' Vision tumbled from Eliab's mouth in an ecstatic jumble of Aramaic and Greek, and the magi whistled their astonishment.

"For centuries we have studied your Hebrew writings as truth," the magus continued. "The scrolls of Moses proclaim: 'A star of Jacob takes leadership; a scepter arises from Israel.' The mesori disappeared before dawn, but we are convinced we saw the scepter of a mighty prince. Upon arriving in Jerusalem we learned that your prophets identified this little town as the birthplace of a great ruler!" Kavir-Meshed's voice was growing loud with anticipation. "He is here, Eliab! Do you know where we can find Him and pay Him homage?"

Suddenly the flickering ember deep inside Eliab's bosom burst into a raging blaze. "Oh, could it be?" he moaned loudly. Tears squirted from between the crevices of his huge cheeks as he confessed his disbelief and greed, as if seeking absolution from the holy man before him.

"Yes, I can take you to him!" Eliab proclaimed jubilantly as he struggled to his feet.

Shortly before sunset a little boy stood in the doorway of His parents' house near the edge of town. His arms and legs were soiled from a day of play, and a sprinkle of sawdust crowned His curly black hair.

The boy noticed a group of men walking toward the house. When they saw the Child, the five most colorfully robed visitors knelt worshipfully in the dirt and placed brightly decorated boxes and bags at the toddler's feet. A short fat man in commoner's garb also eased himself to his knees and lowered his forehead to the earth. With outstretched arms he pushed a bulging black satchel toward the Child.

FOR THOUGHT AND DISCUSSION

1. Describe your idea of what Joseph, Mary, and the infant Jesus might have looked like at the time of this story?
2. Read Matt. 2:1-12. What evidence do you see in the account of the magi that these individuals were believers, not skeptics?
3. If you had been living in Bethlehem at the time of Christ's birth, would you have been a skeptic or a believer at hearing the account of the Shepherds' Vision? Why?
4. What elements of your Christian life are well-fortified with faith? What areas are tainted with skepticism?

4

SECOND WIND

"ALL RUNNERS TO THE STARTING LINE!" The command blared from a bullhorn somewhere near the banner draped over Second Street, which read, "SUMMERFEST TWILIGHT RUN." Tannis Corey found enough room in the jostling throng to allow her lean five-foot, five-inch frame a few more deep knee bends and hamstring stretches.

Tannis spied her husband, Mike, several runners to her left and wished him luck with a smiling wink. The crack of the starter's pistol shot echoed loudly against the marble courthouse, and Tannis gingerly began trotting behind 60 bobbing heads. She couldn't help but smile as she passed under the banner and pinched her stopwatch to life. Two 5-kilometer laps—looping from the center of town into the country and back again—were ahead of her. She yearned to be free from the confining crowd and to run unhindered on the open road.

By the time the Summerfest runners had reached the one mile mark, the bobbing mass had stretched to about 20 small packs, each one gliding and panting together rhythmically. Tannis and Mike found each other and ran together for several blocks. Mike was not as dedicated or well-trained as Tannis. She knew that she would soon pull ahead of her husband in order to maintain her aggressive, preplanned pace.

The fact that the Coreys were still running together—and even living together—was an obvious miracle. Only two years earlier their relationship was at a marriage-threatening low ebb. *If it wasn't for Rosie,* Tannis thought as she flicked a quick smile at her husband, *Mike wouldn't be here with me.* "I love you," he puffed loudly enough for her ears only as she began to pull away.

Shortly after turning onto the rural road the clumps of runners thinned to a line perforated by elongated gaps. Tannis began passing some of the slower entrants who were running only one 5K lap. Looking ahead Tannis recognized the laboring gait and slightly overweight form of her friend Rosie Shoop who had started the race near the front of the pack. "You're doing great, Rosie," Tannis encouraged as she overtook her friend. "Don't let up. Keep pressing. This will be your best 5K ever."

"Thanks, Coach," Rosie panted, her face flushed to a dull crimson. "See you at the finish line."

Where would we be without Rosie and Gary? Tannis wondered as she paced herself between runners. A few days after Tannis, Mike, and their 10-year-old daughter, Trixie, had moved into their house, the Shoops, living across the street, came over with a heaping plate of snickerdoodles and a warm welcome to the neighborhood. During the next months the two couples became casual friends—borrowing cups of sugar and reciprocating invitations to dinner and games. Soon the Coreys had infected the older and less athletic Shoops with their interest in running. Gary and Rosie attended a few races to stand with Trixie while her parents ran. Then Rosie began running alongside Tannis during her daily workouts.

Late one Saturday night in the Shoops' family room, after a day of running and an evening of chicken chow mein, Mike and Tannis painfully confided that they were not getting along. Running was a common interest, they confessed, but everything else about them was uncommon and divisive.

The Coreys weren't aware that their friends had been praying for just such a moment of vulnerability. After Tannis and Mike had emptied their hearts, Gary and Rosie lovingly told their neighbors how Jesus had healed their marriage. After several evenings of discussion, the Coreys knelt beside the Shoops and offered their lives and crumbling marriage to Christ.

Thank You, Jesus, Tannis reflected as she ran alone on the country lateral. She blinked away a tear of gratitude.

It was Rosie who pushed her to keep her relationship with God fresh and vital. "Life in Christ is like a race," Rosie would lecture. "If you don't stay in shape daily by actively pursuing spiritual victory, you'll give out in the heat of the race."

As Tannis veered off the country road and onto State Street, she was surprised by an insight that made her smile in spite of the fatigue that dogged her in the midsummer heat. I coach Rosie in running and push her to stay in shape. And she coaches me to remain consistent in my relationship with the Lord. *You gave me a great coach,* Tannis puffed heavenward, eyes watery again.

The heat radiating from the asphalt lapped at Tannis' strength as she ran down State Street toward the center of town. She rounded Second Street to the encouraging applause of a thin crowd of onlookers. As she passed under the banner for the second time and glanced at her watch, Tannis realized that she was within range of breaking her personal 10K record of 46 minutes.

But after reaching the sunbathed country road Tannis' breathing became more labored. She was painfully aware that she was approaching her major antagonist on the 10K—the seven-kilometer "wall." Her lungs clamored for more air than she could suck in. Her arms drooped from her shoulders as if they were cast in lead. Her legs seemed to detach themselves from her torso and run in slow motion.

But the biggest challenge of hitting the wall was the mental torture. *You'll never make it!* her thoughts taunted her. *Walk! Rest! Give up!* "Mechanics, mechanics, mechanics," Tannis chanted to her rebellious body. Tannis knew that if she could keep the mechanics together—arms pumping rhythmically, legs gliding, feet stepping—she would soon catch her second wind and finish strongly.

Here again, the race paralleled Tannis' spiritual journey. As beautifully as her spiritual trek had begun, Tannis had already hit the wall in her infant relationship with Christ. As soon as her faith budded, Tannis knew she needed to rekindle a long-neglected concern for her mother, a lonely, often-depressed divorcée. So Tannis began visiting her and calling her, but the young woman's kindness was seldom acknowledged. Instead Tannis' mother seemed to withdraw further as if offended by the new beauty her daughter exuded. Then one evening Tannis found her mother dead beside an empty bottle of barbiturates.

Tannis was devastated. She bitterly blamed God for letting it happen and cursed herself for many years of love lost. Tannis' spiritual lungs gasped for air in the stifling heat of the test. A dark spectator in the shadows jeered at her to quit.

But like a good coach, Rosie was beside her with encouragement. "Life's disappointments are like the fatigue that turns your legs to Jell-O. It goes with the race. Do you give up each time you hit the wall?"

Tannis shook her bowed head softly. "I'm tempted to sometimes, but I always tough it out and finish."

"It's not much different running with the Lord," Rosie continued supportively, her arm around Tannis' shoulders. "He's running beside you and will give you your second wind if you keep faithfully pressing on." And after several days of coaching and tearful prayer Tannis *did* catch her second wind and resumed her determined run with Jesus.

Run with me now, Lord, Tannis couldn't even form the words on her lips as she drove herself through the oppressive seventh kilometer. A wave of courage washed over her. She felt her strength and rhythm return. Second wind! she exulted.

Once on State Street Tannis ran with renewed vigor. Unless I break a leg, Tannis calculated with a glance at her watch, I can beat my record by more than a minute!

The gathering crowds urged Tannis on with applause and cheers. Her hair flopped limply around her saturated sweatband. Her arms and legs glistened with perspiration, and her yellow top was splotched with moisture. For a split second Tannis glimpsed beyond the curbside spectators and saw the Giver of the Second Wind applauding her too.

FOR THOUGHT AND DISCUSSION

1. What characteristics and deeds of Rosie Shoop were the most helpful to Tannis in her young Christian life?
2. Read Phil. 3:12-14. What qualities from these verses are needed when tough experiences plague Christians?
3. Why are Christians often reticent to confide in one another with their problems and prayer needs?
4. Who is the "Rosie" in your life—an individual who has encouraged you and stood by you through tough times? For whom are you presently serving as a "Rosie"?

5

THE PANCAKE MEMOS

TO: Rev. Donald Dunmartin, Pastor
Seedy Valley Community Church
FROM: Roland Bixby, Committee Chairman
Annual Memorial Day Pancake Breakfast
RE: Summary Report

AS YOU KNOW, PASTOR, the Annual Memorial Day Pancake Breakfast is the biggest event on our church calendar. We involve more people in planning, promoting, decorating, cooking, dishing up, and serving than a year's worth of choir cantatas, senior citizens' luncheons, and youth socials combined. We use more space in the fellowship hall than the Missionary Sewing Circle could cover with quilts in a decade. And we attract more non-Christians from the community than at Christmas, Easter, and Mother's Day combined.

All of us on the committee were deeply disappointed that you were unable to attend this year due to your sudden illness. But I have good news! This year's breakfast was another smashing success, as evidenced in yesterday's edition of the *Seedy Valley Sentinel.* Religion editor Moshe Feldstein (who, by the way, is a personal friend of mine) stated, "This year's version of Community Church's pancake extravaganza totally outclassed First Baptist's spaghetti feed and United Methodist's strawberry shortcake festival in the community's fund-raising circuit." You may be interested to learn, Pastor, that Moshe gave a $10.00 donation even though he did not take any ham, bacon, or sausage.

It was in last year's article, I might humbly add, that Mr. Feldstein recognized my able leadership of this annual event by referring to me in his story as the Pharaoh of Flapjack, a title I have endeavored to live up to.

The chief value of our annual breakfast is, of course, the image that we present to the community through our efforts. In a town like ours with more churches than taverns, it is important to impress the citizens with our efficiency and relevance in the religious community. There are enough bizarre cults and weirdo sects around that fracture the credibility of Christianity among the general population. We must continually unfurl the banner of respectability and tradition in opposition to the religious crazies who infest our culture.

The Annual Pancake Breakfast is a primary way to hoist the flag of respectability on our corner. After all, when did our Lord attract His greatest following? When He fed the multitudes, of course! Who knows how many of them might have taken after some mystical, pantheistic guru if Jesus hadn't attracted them with a respectable and traditional meal of bread and fish? In our day and age, we are doing the same thing with pancakes and sausage.

Speaking of the menu, if we are to uphold our position of prominence in the community we must improve our menu in the coming year. Respectability and tradition notwithstanding, our good old American flapjacks are losing ground to the upstart fast-food breakfasts. Let's face it: A soggy, mealy pancake can't hold a candle to a Mr. Eggface sandwich. And how many from the Saturday morning cartoon crowd would be lured away from a bowl of Sparkly

Fruit Crunchies (with a treasure map maze on the back of the box and a Captain Starblast ring inside) by a generic pancake? Upward and onward, Pastor! We're talking waffles, blintzes, and pop-up toaster tarts. In my opinion, unless we diversify our menu we are dead in the syrup.

All in all, last Saturday's breakfast seemed to be a great success if I do say so myself. I personally supervised most aspects of the event even though I was unable to get involved in the manual labor due to recurring allergies and chronic back trouble. But then it's biblical for the pharaoh to sit in his chariot while the soldiers do all the fighting, right? I've always tried to be a biblical leader.

Incidentally, there was a new guy poking around the church during the breakfast—named Curly or Burly or something—who looked rather suspicious. He was volunteering for all the jobs that got him close to our people. He may be from another church trying to proselyte from our congregation. Just before I left the dining hall to attend the parade I saw him fraternizing with Mr. Frick, that crusty church janitor of yours. Anybody attracted to sour old Frick bears watching.

As you can see from my report, I am deeply committed to the success of this annual event. As such, I humbly toss my hat (along with my record of success in the breakfast just completed) into the ring for nomination as chairman of next year's committee. My work schedule is such that I can donate the required amount of time to the job, providing I may again deduct the monetary value of time volunteered from my offerings. My experience in leadership is great, and my influence in the community is even greater: City Planning Commission, Junior Chamber, Moose Lodge. In fact, it would be difficult to imagine the continuing success of the breakfast without my influence on the community leaders I touch every day. Besides, as Moshe Feldstein told me privately, pharaohs are appointed for life, if you catch my drift.

Yours for a bigger and better Breakfast,
Roland "The Pharaoh of Flapjack" Bixby

TO: Pastor Donald Dunmartin at Community Church
(Hope you're feeling better. We missed you!)

FROM: Monalisa Vargas, Treasurer
Annual Pancake Breakfast

RE: Financial Report

PLEASE FIND ATTACHED a detailed accounting of the receipts and expenditures for our most recent Annual Memorial Day Breakfast. For the most part the figures speak for themselves. But please allow me to comment on a few items from the perspective of financial management.

First, as you can plainly see on page 3, we undershot our goal again this year. In spite of careful planning, we netted only $560 instead of the $800 we had anticipated. There are several reasons for our failure, most of them predictable. Pancake flour and syrup went up this year, as did bacon and juice. Furthermore, though several people donated more than the suggested amount, an even greater number refused to give any money at all, insisting that a donation meal is a complimentary meal. And these people ate twice as much as those who donated money.

There is another reason we did so poorly at the donation table, Pastor. I hesitate to mention it except that I feel partly responsible for the financial success or failure of the breakfast. I was given several hand-lettered cards that morning, which were made by a member of our committee who shall remain nameless. The bearers of these cards were members of the City Planning Commission, Junior Chamber, and Moose Lodge. Each card read: "Community Church Annual Pancake Breakfast—Complimentary Ticket." The cards were signed, "The Pharaoh." From my observations, these people, who could have contributed generously, even out-ate the nondonor types.

Second, you can see by my count that our attendance was down slightly this year even though our publicity committee spent more money. I'm afraid that what we gained in quantity of publicity we lost in quality, which contributed to the decline in attendance. It seems that, among the reader boards our committee secured this year, the breakfast was advertised on the marquee of the local theater. Several of our parishioners were incensed that the announcement of the breakfast appeared just below the title of the currently running film. Perhaps less money and more discretion will be in order for the publicity committee next year.

Phong Nguyen, the publicity chairman, told me that they never would have reached their goals if not for an energetic young man who spent two days delivering posters to the stores in town. Because the young man is new to our church, I don't know his name, but Nguyen said that he was different from the other committee members. He *volunteered* to help instead of being arm-wrestled into it.

Finally, Pastor, the major purpose of this annual affair, as I see it, is to raise money for the church budget. If so, we must marshal our efforts to the maximum to achieve this goal. For example, we should serve smaller portions and use the cheapest brands possible. Additionally, we should print the word *donation* in smaller letters on the posters and tickets, perhaps in light yellow ink. If we can make people think that payment is required, we will support fewer freeloaders. Also, somebody needs to talk to "The Pharaoh" about his back-slapping generosity. Complimentary tickets are uncomplimentary to our success.

Speaking of uncomplimentary, I received a nasty telephone call Saturday night from Mr. Frick the janitor. He chewed me out about the condition of the dining hall and kitchen after the breakfast. I told him that if *we* cleaned up after the breakfast, there would be no reason to pay *him.* I couldn't understand what he said next, but it's probably just as well. I think he needs a reprimand, Pastor.

Respectfully submitted,
Monalisa Vargas

TO: Pastor Donald Dunmartin at the church
FROM: Daisy Kowalski, Kitchen Chairman
Annual Church Breakfast
RE: Kitchen equipment and supplies

BEFORE YOU HEAR any complaints about last weekend's breakfast, Pastor, I want you to know that it wasn't my fault. The equipment in our church is so bad that even Wonder Woman couldn't have done better than we did—which was pretty bad—under the same conditions. We'll never reach our goal of providing a nutritious, delicious breakfast until we do something about that kitchen.

Since the church still does not own a commercial griddle, we again cooked several hundred pancakes on a collection of electric frypans we have accumulated over the years. Some of the pans are OK, but most of them don't work very well at all. Fredericka Spooner received three or four shocks from the skillet she was using, putting an extra curl in her red hair. And Charlie Bickwood made several trips to the basement flipping breakers back on from the overloaded circuits. Some of the skillets only worked on one side of the frying surface. As a result, the pancakes we served to Mayor Eppincott looked like the moon halfway between new and full: charcoal black on the left side and gooey white on the right.

If we cannot install a commercial griddle by next year, we should at least invest in some large household griddles like I have at home. They handle twice as many pancakes as a kitchen skillet and are much easier to clean. I decided not to bring my griddle last Saturday because I didn't want any unnecessary scratches on the nonstick surface.

We also need some nice plastic pitchers for mixing batter. Our cooks mixed batter in an old coffee urn and scooped it onto the skillets with cereal bowls. It was a real mess! Most of the pancakes looked like something from the Roarshark (or whatever his name is) ink spot test. One lady ran crying from the dining hall because the pancake on her plate resembled her cat Muffy, which was killed by a truck two weeks ago.

We should have a supply of pitchers like the three I have at home. Of course, I could not bring them to the church breakfast because they might have been broken or stolen.

Perhaps next year we should not use as many teenagers as cooks. During the busiest part of the morning our teen crew decided to go to the parade early. We would have been up a creek without a spatula if it hadn't been for a friendly young man who saw the unattended pancakes on the range and stepped in to pick up the slack. I was going to thank him as we all walked to the parade after breakfast, but he was nowhere to be seen.

One last thing on equipment, Pastor. The automatic dishwasher needs an adjustment. The water jets were spraying so hard that they shattered every plate in the first load. We left the broken pieces in the dishwasher and the unwashed dishes stacked on the sink. We figured the janitor would clean up after us.

Yours truly,
Daisy

TO: Rev. Dunmartin
FROM: Burton Frick, Church Janitor
RE: My resignation from this job

IT IS WITH A LITTLE bit of sad and a whole heap of mad that I quit the job of church janitor—which I have held faithfully for the past 17 years—effective right now, today! Please send my last paycheck to my home as I won't darken the door of your church again. My wife and I have also cancelled our plans to become church members, which we have thought about for the past 10 years.

Over the years of my work here I have put up with lots of nonsense and trouble in your church. Every week some fool kid in the Sunday School stomps clay into the carpet.

Other kids write on walls, spill glue on the tables, and smear finger paints on the supply cabinets.

And your crazy youth pastor and his teenagers have kept me awake nights with their messes of popcorn, shaving cream, and cookie crumbs in the youth lounge. And you can find their chewing gum in the awfulest and most sacred places. I can handle all this most of the time.

But the thing that has lit my cork for the last time is the annual fiasco you call the Memorial Day Pancake Breakfast. Thanks to this church I will never be able to eat pancakes again, because the thought of them makes me break out in nervous hives.

You may be asking, "What do you mean by that, Mr. Frick?" so I'll tell you, Reverend. First, I mean that in 17 years I have never had a Memorial Day off. In fact, it has been the longest day of the year because of your Pancake Breakfast. After the breakfast is over at eleven o'clock, your committee, led by that lazy chairman Bixby, sneaks off to the Memorial Day Parade—which I have never seen in 17 years—and doesn't come back.

If you would have been there last Saturday after the breakfast (I'm sorry you weren't feeling well), you would have found me in a kitchen covered with enough grease to lube a fleet of tanks. Also, the frypans were corroded with petrified bacon and pancake batter, the floors (7,000 square feet of them!) were sticky with orange juice and syrup, and there was enough garbage to fill the dumpster three times over. And then to top off the whole day, I discovered the dishwasher full of broken china and the sinks piled high with dishes that I am supposed to wash. I am not ashamed to admit that there were a few more broken dishes that day than I originally found in the dishwasher.

Now I've never been afraid of hard work, and I still ain't. I come from a branch of the family tree that was raised on hard work. And just as important as getting your own chores done was helping the rest of the family with their chores. As my sainted mother—who has been dead 27 years

—always said, "No one is done until the last one is done."

What really pops my fuse is that you preach the same thing, Reverend: love one another, serve one another, help those that need help, be a servant, and the like. But all I see at your breakfast is a bunch of lazy chiefs who don't care a hoot about helping. They are only interested in getting a crowd to the breakfast so they can make lots of money for the church and impress their snooty friends. But they can't see past the ends of their noses in the air to where old Burton Frick is standing in need of their help once in awhile. There may be some servants in that parish of yours, but I don't see any of them at your Pancake Breakfast.

Oh, I guess I should take that at least part ways back. There was one young fellah—I forget his name—who stayed behind to help after everybody else left for the parade. He picked all broken china out of the dishwasher and seemed to enjoy scrubbing grease off the walls. I wonder how he ever got involved in your church!

Anyway, I'm gone.
Sincerely as I can be,
Burton Frick, ex-janitor

TO: Pastor Donald Dunmartin
FROM: Matt Hurley, Committeeman-at-Large
Annual Memorial Day Pancake Breakfast
RE: A word of thanks

YOU PROBABLY DON'T know me because I am fairly new to Seedy Valley. I began attending Community Church about three months ago. I was hoping to meet you personally at the Breakfast, but I understand you were ill on Saturday. I hope you are feeling better now.

When I heard about the Pancake Breakfast provided for the community by the church I became excited about helping out. The chairman—I think somebody called him Mr. Farrow—said all the major jobs were taken, but I could serve on the committee-at-large and help wherever I was needed. I was thrilled to be a part of the team!

I first worked with the publicity committee distributing posters. It was great to visit all the stores in town and spread the word about the breakfast. I met so many nice people and told them all about our church.

Next, I heard that the decorations committee was a little short-handed so I offered to help them. Most everybody else was more artistic than I, so they hung the red, white, and blue crepe paper and cardboard flags while I mopped the floors, wiped the tables, and polished the stainless. What a feeling of accomplishment!

I didn't have a specific job during the breakfast itself, so I did several things. A couple of the coffee hostesses didn't show up, so I circulated among the tables for a while filling coffee cups. I was also able to flip some pancakes, make orange juice, and bus tables. Everywhere I worked I met new people. What great fellowship!

After the breakfast most of the crew had to meet their families at the parade. So I stayed around and helped Mr. Frick put the place back together. He's a sweet old gentleman once you get past his gruff exterior. I enjoyed working with him.

I could see right from the start that the focal point of the Pancake Breakfast was ministry to the community. Our church ministered to the people of Seedy Valley by providing a delicious, low-cost breakfast prior to the holiday parade. In so doing we were able to meet some people who might never come to church. I thank God that I had an opportunity to share the love of Christ that way.

And thank *you* for allowing me, a newcomer, to minister to the Lord and the church. I hope I didn't rob someone else of a chance to serve by taking on the projects I did. It's just that I have committed my life to serve Christ and His church in whatever ways I can. I'm not a preacher or a teacher, and I can't sing more than two notes on either side of monotone. But somehow I find plenty of things that need to be done every day. I find the greatest joy in knowing I have helped meet somebody's need in some way.

Please let me know what else I can do for you.

At your service,
Matt Hurley

P.S.: MR. FRICK WAS PRETTY discouraged about his workload at the breakfast, and he grumbled something about quitting. Don't take him too seriously. I'm going over to his house next Saturday to help him snake out his drains and gutters. (He is not as nimble as he once was, so I volunteered to give him a hand.) I'm also going to start helping him around the church a couple of afternoons each week—strictly as a volunteer. I think with some encouragement and assistance he might change his mind about quitting.

FOR THOUGHT AND DISCUSSION

1. Each memo writer had a different perspective of the purpose of the church breakfast. What was the perspective of Roland Bixby? Monalisa Vargas? Daisy Kowalski? Burton Frick? Matt Hurley?
2. Read John 13:3-17. What attitude was Jesus demonstrating to His disciples? How did He demonstrate it?
3. Of your acquaintances, who best demonstrates the attitude of Matt Hurley? How do they do so?
4. Which of the five characters in the story reminds you most of your response to service opportunities?

6

PURSUED BY LOVE

THERE I WAS, alone in the near-darkness. Blood was dripping from my lip. My gown was torn and dangling in twisted pieces from my shoulders and waist. There wasn't one inch of me, inside or out, that didn't hurt.

I dreaded the pounding mental and emotional hangover that always followed a bad night. How I hated selling myself to men in the name of Baal worship!

The shadows in my room smothered me, and the bitter pungency of the incense candles thrust their suffocating fumes into my throat. I cursed and screamed and bawled. I huddled, shivering on my bed like a mortally wounded animal, wishing again that my lord Baal would pity me and end my life.

Suddenly a man was in the doorway, a dark silhouette against the torchlight that illuminated the hallway behind him.

"Gomer?" His voice searched the dark cavern of my room. I gasped so deeply at the voice that I gagged and coughed. I have been called by many names within the temple walls, some of them even *I* am embarrassed to repeat. But I had not been called by my real name in almost two years. The man in the doorway was my husband.

It was about 6 years ago that Hosea, my husband, approached my father to contract our marriage. I was barely 15 at the time, but I had already been initiated into the rites of temple worship by several of my lord Baal's priests.

No one was more surprised than my father when Hosea, a prophet of Jehovah, approached him with the bride price. By Jehovah's standards I was considered "damaged goods"—an adulterous woman worthy only of a heap of stones large enough to bury me! But my opportunistic father gladly took the money and turned me over to Hosea, who led me proudly to his home as if I was the queen of Sheba.

The children came quickly—a son, then a daughter, then another son. I had every reason to be content. But after several years, Hosea was spending greater amounts of time away from home proclaiming Jehovah's unconditional love for His faithless people. I was left at home with the babies.

It was during one of his journeys away that Baal's priests came to our town offering tempting treasures to girls who would serve as temple priestesses. The sparkling jewelry looked much more appealing than my simple life. And the jeweled gowns were more attractive than my nursing robe.

I let myself believe that serving in Baal's temple would be a spiritual act that would somehow even please Hosea, my fervent prophet-husband. So in a moment of subtly blinding delusion, I left my babies and joined the harem.

Yes, Hosea had been a good husband. I wasn't running from him. I was running to the glitter of Baal's treasures. Hosea never showed me anything but respect and tenderness, which I had all but forgotten until he appeared at the door last night.

When I gasped and coughed, he called into the dark haze again. "Gomer, my wife, are you in there?" His voice was at once both authoritative and gentle.

I felt an avalanche of shame rush over me and reached for a blanket to cover myself. My body had been exploited by countless strange men, but when Hosea appeared at my door I covered up. I hadn't felt such shame since the first day I came to the temple as a child.

"Get out of here!" I pushed at him in a low voice, half of me repulsing the disarming love that radiated from him, half of me wishing he would speak my name again.

"Gomer, it is you!" he interrupted me. His voice was deep and coarse from the strain of impassioned preaching, but his tone revealed the innocent joy of a shepherd boy finding a lost lamb in the wild.

"I am Hosea, your husband." He stepped into the room and lifted one of the candles to his weathered, bearded face. The flame seemed to ricochet from his dark eyes, disintegrating the shields I frantically tried to lift in defense.

"You should not be here, Hosea," I was almost crying. "I'm not the same girl you bartered for. I am not your wife. I am a slave now. I am owned by Baal." The words were rancid in my mouth.

"Gomer, my loved one, you are not a slave any longer," Hosea's words flowed sweet and warm with confidence. "I have longed for you and searched for you since you went away," his voice began to quaver and small tears formed in the corners of his eyes, glistening in the candlelight.

"Jehovah brought me to your door tonight. You will now come with me to our home and our children," he insisted expectantly.

Many men have swaggered in and bellowed their demands. But Hosea's words came as an invitation to a banquet in my honor for which there was no reasonable cause to refuse.

"But Hosea, I am worthless!" I almost screamed. The love that poured out from my husband rose around me as a violent tide, and I began to tremble. "Don't you realize that? I am a . . ."

He was kneeling at the bedside with his hand gently stopping the words at my lips. "You are my wife. I have loved you. I do love you. I have searched for you, and I have found you. You will come and serve me and enjoy my home again."

Like a dam crumbling inside me, the floodwaters gushed from my eyes in tears of sorrow, shame, and joy. I was a ship gliding at last into a quiet, secure harbor after a perilous voyage on life-threatening seas. Amid the sobs came words I never expected to say to any man again, but that bathed my soul with peace: "Yes, my lord."

When the weeping had subsided, Hosea took a soft cloth from the basin by the door and carefully washed the dried blood and smeared makeup from my face. Then he pulled a neatly folded garment from inside his sash and held it out to me. "This will keep you warm on our way home," he smiled. Then he stepped from the room while I dressed.

The garment was a beautiful white robe, custom made for a new bride. I have never been more proud of anything I've owned.

FOR THOUGHT AND DISCUSSION

1. This fictitious story is based on Hos. 1:1-9; 3:1. List the various emotions Gomer experienced through the course of this story.
2. Read Hos. 1:2. How is marital promiscuity and unfaithfulness an apt illustration of spiritual unfaithfulness?
3. What are some common temptations to spiritual infidelity that Christians face today?
4. Who or what is God's greatest rival for supremacy in your life today?

7

MONEY TO BURN

MITCH VAUGHN JERKED UPRIGHT in bed at the faint smell of smoke in the predawn darkness. His ears tuned to the whistle of a strong wind outside and the crackle of wood on fire. His eyes focused on an orange glow flickering behind the bedroom curtains.

"Jeri! Fire!" Mitch alarmed his sleeping wife with an urgent jostle, then bounded to the window and swept the curtains aside. "Oh, no, it's the garage!" he shouted, reaching for his jeans. "Call the emergency number! And call Ken Edwards! I'll get the hose."

Mitch raced down the stairway and out the side door to the garage, which was almost encircled by flame driven from a fierce east wind. The roar of the ravenous blaze made him gasp with fright, and the searing heat pushed him away from the structure and its valuable contents.

"Our Blazer! Our new boat!" Mitch moaned as he launched a feeble stream of water from the garden hose into the inferno. The crackling fire was unaffected by the inadequate amount of water. After two minutes Mitch reluctantly turned the spray from its unquenchable target to the shake roof of his house, which was being peppered with live embers.

Suddenly Mitch noticed a frightening orange ball of flame looming behind his garage, filling the sky above him with billows of smoke and swirling embers. "That's Andrew's place!" he shouted. "It's going up like a bonfire!"

Ken Edwards, Mitch's neighbor on the adjacent acre, screeched his pick-up to a stop in Vaughn's driveway. "What can I do?" he shouted above the deafening roar as he ran toward Mitch.

"The garage is gone," Mitch lamented, handing Ken the hose. "Keep pouring water on the house. I'm going to see about Andrew."

Mitch sprinted to the back of his lot and vaulted the privacy fence enclosing his yard. Andrew Bell, a widower in his early 70s, lived alone in his tiny, wood frame house behind the Vaughns. He occupied his days tending a large garden and passed his evenings watching television, always with a bottle of beer within reach. Andrew had been generally unresponsive to Mitch and Jeri's attempts at friendship, but he did have a soft spot in his heart for their two daughters, 11-year-old Carla and 6-year-old Tippy.

Mitch was relieved to find Andrew standing a safe distance behind his blazing cottage. The gusting wind rippled the old man's flannel nightshirt and stood his thin white hair on end. He cradled a half-empty quart of beer in one arm.

"Are you all right, Andrew?" Mitch quizzed his neighbor, whose eyes remained fixed on the brilliant yellow flames enveloping his house.

"The wind snapped a power line out front," Andrew moaned absently. "Must have touched off the brush around my house, then *whoosh*—there goes my house!" Mitch noted the windy course the sparks followed from Andrew's burning house to the dry brush behind his garage. "The dogs woke me up barking like crazy, but now I almost wish they hadn't." Andrew's voice trailed off to a sad whimper and was overpowered by the wailing sirens of the fire trucks approaching both burning buildings.

"Don't worry, Andrew." Mitch wrapped a compassionate arm around the old man's shoulders. "I have some clothes you can wear. Everything will be OK." Andrew sighed and nodded.

Mitch found his wife and daughters huddled on the porch steps watching the firemen pump a hissing waterfall on the blaze. He assured them of Andrew's safety.

"Daddy, our bikes are in there!" Tippy sobbed, pointing to the smoldering skeleton of charred wood and metal silhouetted by the dawn of light. Jeri was also misty-eyed as she itemized their loss: the Chevy Blazer, their new ski boat, the girls' bikes, and Mitch's tools and golf clubs.

Carla added her complaint, listing personal treasures in the garage that had been gobbled up by the flames: "My own water skis and life jacket. And my doll stroller."

Mitch extended arms of comfort to his distressed family. "Let's look on the bright side, girls. Thanks to the Lord, we are all safe. And our insurance covers full replacement value of everything we've lost." His three ladies seemed only slightly consoled, as was Mitch. "Now you girls prepare the guest room while I go pick up Andrew and his dogs. We have some orphans to take care of."

By 9:30 A.M. Andrew and his two dogs, Buster and Charlie, were sleeping off the previous night's trauma in the guest room. Carla and Tippy were in the backyard exaggerating the details of the fire to their friends. And Mitch and Jeri sat at the kitchen counter with cups of fresh coffee.

"The insurance man will be here today to fill out a claim report," Mitch said. "I told him we have a detailed inventory of the garage's contents. He said we should have a check within a week or so. I figure it will amount to about $40,000."

Jeri whistled at the figure, then voiced their previously unspoken concern. "But what are we going to do with Andrew? He wants to be on his own, but where can he go?"

Mitch stirred his thoughts along with his coffee. "Andrew has no children or other relatives. And he has no insurance on that old house. He has his land, two dogs, and a nightshirt—that's it! Like it or not, he's stuck with us—and we're stuck with him—until God shows us what to do."

"But Andrew doesn't want to live with us," Jeri protested. "He has barely spoken 25 words to us in the three years we've known him. And most of those words were refusals to our dinner invitations."

"I know, Babe," Mitch agreed. "But we can't just send him packing when he has no real alternatives. He can't afford a retirement home, and I think he'd rather die than move into the rescue mission in town."

The couple sat silently for several more minutes sipping coffee and searching for solutions. Finally Mitch drained his cup and rose to begin the task of salvaging what he could from the jagged, charred heap that had been their garage. He turned at the kitchen door and voiced an impromptu prayer for both of them. "Lord, we've never done this before," Mitch was staring at the kitchen counter as if Jesus were sitting next to Jeri. "You know our hearts; we want to care for Andrew. We just don't know how to do it. Please give us the wisdom we need."

After a few silent seconds Jeri caught her husband's eye and flashed an affirmative smile. "Amen," she said.

After a distressing day of picking through his charred possessions and grumbling about his fate, Andrew retired to the guest room after supper. Carla and Tippy joined their parents in the bedroom for evening prayers.

Both girls asked God to replace the things lost in the fire. Their lists were detailed and accurate down to the color of "socks" on Mitch's golf club heads. But Mitch and Jeri were pleased by Carla and Tippy's prayerful concern for Andrew Bell—and for Buster and Charlie. Their prayers were rich in childlike faith.

"Is Andrew gonna live with us till he dies?" Tippy asked innocently after her father had pronounced the last amen.

"Oh, brother!" Carla groaned, embarrassed by her sister's curiosity. Mitch flicked Carla a look that meant "cool it." Jeri tried to answer Tippy's question.

"Sweetie, Andrew has lived alone so long that he really doesn't want to live with us or anybody. He wants to live on his own land in his own house. But now that's impossible."

The conversation progressed two or three sentences into another topic, but Tippy's young mind was still wrestling with Andrew's dilemma. Tippy's eyes suddenly widened, signaling the flash of a childish solution. "We could buy Andrew another house and put it by his burned house. We could use our thousands-of-dollars 'surance check."

Carla flopped back on the bed mimicking a dead faint. "You're crazy! That money is so we can buy a new boat and bikes and stuff."

But Tippy persisted with brazen, six-year-old conviction. "Carla, Andrew can't live in a Blazer or a boat. He needs a house like we have. And we should buy him one."

Tippy and Carla continued sparring on the topic, but Mitch and Jeri were speechless. Their eyes were locked together and a bolt of insight passed between them like electricity.

Family time concluded, and each of the parents nuzzled and tickled a daughter as part of their bedtime ritual. When the girls had finally been tucked in for the night, Mitch and Jeri returned to the family room. Each of them knew that Tippy's simple suggestion was the key to their solution for Andrew Bell. But neither of them wanted to initiate the discussion. Mitch flipped through the channels on the TV while Jeri disinterestedly leafed through a couple of magazines.

Later that night it was Mitch who finally broke the silence as he and Jeri lay in the darkness. "I think I heard God speaking to us in the voice of a six-year old child."

Jeri's sigh was audible. "I was wishing you wouldn't say that, but I think I heard the same thing."

They talked about how much they had enjoyed their four-by-four, ski boat, and other nice things God had allowed them to own. They convinced each other that they had worked hard and saved long for their things while Andrew Bell had irresponsibly guzzled his resources.

They reminded each other of the marriage-long commitment they shared to love God and use things, and never to flip-flop the two verbs. But they calculated that providing some kind of housing for Andrew would leave them only enough cash to rebuild the garage and little more. They painfully agreed that, even though they already supported their church and missions, God had simultaneously plopped in their laps both a mission field and the means for serving that field.

They discussed their alternatives and plotted a course of action. Then they slipped to their knees to pray. Jeri wept and Mitch sniffled as he uttered the last words of the night: "Lord, help us to love Andrew Bell."

Andrew thought there was all too much cheeriness around the Vaughn household over the next several days in the light of the loss they had suffered. "What's everybody so happy about?" the old man groused.

Construction had begun on the new garage and all activity seemed to make Andrew grumpier than ever. He escaped across the fence to his garden often and welcomed the hours of silence in the house when the Vaughns traveled into town. He was secretly irritated that he wasn't invited to ride into town with them, although he would have refused the invitations with a snorting, "Nope."

The day after the insurance check arrived, Andrew was whisked into the family car for a trip into town in spite of his grumpy protestation. The girls' persistence about a "big surprise" quieted his fuming to mild tolerance.

After 10 minutes of driving, Mitch steered to the curb in front of King's Coaches, a mobile home dealership. In the driveway, hitched to a truck, was an older single-wide mobile home.

"C'mon, Andrew, I want you to meet a friend of mine," Mitch was pointing to the man in the doorway of the trailer.

Annoyed by another interruption in his day, Andrew stepped out of the backseat with Carla and Tippy at his heels.

"Andrew, this is Ben King." The man in the doorway stepped down and grasped Andrew's hand. "Mr. King is going to deliver this mobile home to 29956 Abelia Road. Would you ride along and show him how to get there?"

Andrew bristled. "That's a mistake, because 29956 Abelia Road is my old place, and I don't . . ."

Andrew's explanation was stifled by a quartet singing, "Surprise!"

It took several seconds for all the tumblers to click into place in Andrew's understanding. He looked at Ben King, the coach, and the beaming family. His mouth dropped open and his eyes brimmed with tears. "Oh, not for me!" his words protested. But subconsciously his hands came together in silent, joyful applause.

FOR THOUGHT AND DISCUSSION

1. What are some other ways Mitch and Jeri could have cared for Andrew's need other than buying him a mobile home?
2. Read 2 Cor. 8:7. According to this verse, how important is material giving in comparison to qualities such as faith and love?
3. North American Christians are too materialistic: Do you agree or disagree? Why?
4. Suppose your neighbor suffered a loss similar to that of Andrew Bell. What would you be able to supply to meet the need? What would you be willing to supply?

8

CORRIDORS

I GUESS I'M SO USED to the corridors at our church that I hardly think of them anymore. I'm not talking about the carpeted hallways lined with bulletin boards and tract racks. All churches have corridors like those. I'm referring to these ingenious passageways that cannot be seen or felt. I suppose if they *were* visible our corridors would resemble a maze of giant tunnels made of something in between Plexiglas and Saran Wrap.

Our invisible corridors are tall enough and wide enough for two people to walk abreast, yet they stretch like magic to fit clusters of six or seven people who have gathered to chat. To the ignorant observer our church looks like any other church where people worship, fellowship, and serve together. What the untrained eye cannot detect, however, is that our people worship, fellowship, and serve *only* with those in their own corridor. The unseen corridors keep our congregation members in their proper channels.

Not everyone moves in the same corridor, of course. That's the beauty of the system. Executive Miles Upham, for example, never travels in the same corridor as Buck Waterman, an unemployed bricklayer. Miles' corridor (the same corridor used by most of the businessmen in our congregation) begins in the front lot where he parks his BMW. It winds through the front door and down the center aisle of the sanctuary to a seat in the third row.

Buck, however, parks his ratty-looking Ford pickup in the back lot next to the dumpster. He follows his corridor through an inconspicuous side door to a seat near the back.

The salaried types in Miles' corridor greet one another warmly while standing within inches of the hourly types in Buck's corridor. In fact, the two groups are close enough to speak to each other and embrace each other. But the corridors prevent that from happening.

And you'll never find Cora Snead in the same corridor as Belle Johansson since Belle wouldn't let Cora pitch for the women's softball team. They used to be seen together in the Women's Missionary Society corridor until the incident on the pitcher's mound. That's when Cora migrated to the Chancel Choir corridor, which almost never tracks on the same side of the building as Belle's WMS tunnel.

Also, the members of the Crandall family avoid any corridor containing somebody from the Watson clan. That all started when Elmer Watson beat Floyd Crandall out of a seat on the Deacon Board. Floyd and Elmer were as close as toast and butter in the trustee corridor until Floyd accused Elmer of electioneering at the annual meeting. The last words they uttered to each other were "cheater" and "sore loser." Then Elmer slid proudly into the Deacon Board corridor, and Floyd stomped away toward the Berean class corridor.

As a rule, married couples don't move in the same corridors as singles. The whites and the minorities in the church also congregate in different corridors. And the teenagers and senior citizens usually occupy corridors all others avoid. As you might guess, our corridors have practically eliminated church conflicts.

There once was a rather embarrassing exception, however. A young couple—Tom and Molly Tidewell—visited our church one Sunday. An astute usher spied calluses on

Tom's hands and spit-up stains on Molly's dress and eased the couple into a corridor for blue-collar couples with infants.

But, not perceiving the importance of our corridors, Tom and Molly clumsily crashed through the wall of their corridor, burst into Buck Waterman's corridor, and cordially introduced themselves to Buck and his wife, Julia. Before the appalled ushers could scramble through an adjoining corridor to correct the problem, the Tidewells backtracked. They ripped a hole in another corridor wall and stopped Miles Upham dead in his tracks with "Hi, we're Tom and Molly Tidewell!"

Miles just stood there, mouth frozen open, while Tom pumped his arm enthusiastically. Molly was just about to drag the Watermans through the tattered openings to introduce them to Miles when a panting, wide-eyed usher arrived to remind everyone that the service was beginning. But by this time several other uncouth nonmembers, following Tom and Molly's example, had tramped through the curious openings in the corridors and brashly introduced themselves to practically everybody.

The ushers did a marvelous job manipulating parishioners back into their proper corridors in time for the worship service to begin with its customary reverential decorum. But it took the Deacon Board two hymns, a pastoral prayer, and half of the Gloria Patri to mend the breaches in the corridor walls.

The Tidewells never did get the hang of the corridors, I guess, and they dropped out of sight after two more weeks. The Friendship Committee at the church, chaired by Miles Upham, agreed that Tom and Molly's departure probably prevented an ugly church split.

Pastor Wilson—by the way, he's the only person in the church who has access to all the corridors—preaches often about the importance of fellowship in our church. And I must admit that fellowship is one thing this church does well—thanks to corridors. Miles Upham opens his elegant suburban home once a month to host a lovely buffet dinner for others in his corridor. Buck Waterman and his cronies get together every once in a while for a hobo potluck and bowling. And the Southeast Asians in our church use the Fellowship Hall one Sunday each month for a dinner (but they pay for the paper plates and plastic forks they use).

Frankly, I don't think Pastor Wilson is very fond of the corridors. He probably walks several miles each Sunday just saying hello to everyone. But both the congregation and the corridors were here before he came. I'd hate to see what would happen to our close fellowship—or Pastor Wilson—if the corridors were eliminated.

FOR THOUGHT AND DISCUSSION

1. What do the corridors represent in this allegory? All churches have corridors: Do you agree or disagree? Why?
2. Read Phil. 2:1-5. According to this passage, what is the antidote to the formation of corridors among Christians?
3. What kinds of corridors exist in your church separating believers or groups of believers? How do you think the principles in Phil. 2:1-5 can be effectively applied to the divisions in your church?
4. To what extent are you responsible for promoting or maintaining corridors in your church? What will you do to help remove corridors that currently separate you from others at your church?

9

THE COMMANDER

PASTOR JOSHUA NUNSON'S head was screwed tightly into his pillow, and a technicolor dream bubbled in his brain.

There he was, standing behind the massive oak pulpit in his sanctuary at 12 noon, concluding a dynamic sermon before his congregation of 400. Suddenly he was interrupted by the insistent, shrill beeping of a digital watch strapped to the arm of a young woman sitting in the third row. Pastor Nunson stopped midsentence with mouth gaping as the woman and three friends stood, pulled racquets and tennis balls from the pew racks, and walked to the altar area in front of the platform. With the woman's alarm still screeching impolitely, the quartet began volleying across a net that had mysteriously appeared.

Nunson gripped the pulpit determinedly, glanced at his notes, and pressed on with the sermon's conclusion, his every word punctuated by beeps from the woman's watch and ponks from the optic yellow balls bounding from racquet to racquet in front of him.

He had hardly completed two more sentences when another piercing alarm sounded from the watch of a round, balding man sitting with his wife and three children in the seventh row. When the man's alarm began to blare, a picnic table and barbecue grill suddenly materialized in the side aisle. Nunson stared dumbfounded as the wife and children emptied a picnic basket onto the table and the balding man flopped five big hamburger patties onto the grill, which was already billowing smoke throughout the sanctuary.

Before Pastor Nunson could begin again, another watch beeped, then another, then two more, then four more. With each irritating alarm a handful of parishioners stood and scattered noisily around the sanctuary to picnic tables, barbecue grills, tennis courts, and horseshoe pits that were quickly transforming Jericho Street Church into a city park.

Soon all the chaotic alarms in the sanctuary became a synchronized chorus that grew louder with each succeeding beep. "Honey, shut off our alarm," Trina Nunson called to her husband from the front pew.

"I don't have one of those watches," Nunson bellowed back above the din, extending his left arm toward her, revealing his 12-year-old Timex with a sweep second hand.

"Honey, shut off our alarm," Trina moaned again from under her pillow, jabbing Nunson in the back. The digital clock nagged at him, too, with its relentless beep-beep-beep.

Nunson struggled to poke his arms and legs through the cocoon of semiconsciousness, stumble from the bed to the dresser, fumble for the snooze button, and return to the bedside. But Trina had already rolled to his side of their bed, collected her husband's pillow, and drifted back to sleep.

The pastor sat on the edge of the bed, holding his drooping head in his hands, squinting at the green numerals that glowed in the hazy, dark gray of their bedroom. "6:03," he half-mumbled, half-whispered. "I've got to get up. I've got to go study."

But his memory overpowered his feeble resolve by flashing a fast-forward rerun of the minutes-old dream onto the screen of his barely conscious mind. "Picnic Sunday starring grilled pastor," Nunson captioned the scene cynically. "It would be funny if it weren't so true," he sighed, raking his sparse black hair with his fingers. "They turn me off like a bad commercial if I don't finish by noon."

The dream's image faded and Pastor Nunson's "to do" list crowded into the space behind his grainy lids:

9 A.M.	Staff meeting
10 A.M.	Meet with youth pastor
11 A.M.	Work on visitation program
12 noon	Lunch with deacon chairman

Caleb probably wants to jump me again because of all the people we're losing, the pastor thought as he struggled to keep his eyes open. His afternoon agenda began to blur as a tide of slumber surged steadily up the shore of his dwindling consciousness. Pastor Nunson shook his head sleepily, shuffled to the clock, and switched the alarm to "off."

Rebellious staff, arrogant deacons, apathetic people, and picnic Sunday every week—what's the use! Nunson thought heavily as he scooted his snoring wife to her side of the bed and burrowed himself under the covers. Study time is wasted time, he rationalized, almost enjoying the fresh injection of self-pity.

As the real world began to fade again, the scene of his earlier dream returned. This time the sanctuary was deserted and darkened, littered with the remains of an all-day picnic. Pastor Nunson saw himself standing again at the pulpit wanting desperately to finish his sermon.

Then a figure appeared at the rear center doors of the sanctuary, silhouetted against the faint light streaming in from Jericho Street. Nunson studied the figure curiously as deep sleep began to ebb the scene from his vision. It looks like a man in uniform, he thought.

Seconds before the picture dissolved into oblivion he heard the shadowy figure speak. The dark stranger's words flooded the sanctuary and seemed to sweep around the pastor at the pulpit like a warm current: "Much work requires much worship." Nunson's image tried to ask the figure what he meant, but a giant wave of black silence washed over him, and he was deeply asleep again.

Nunson hurried across the street from the parsonage to the church at 8:55 A.M., disappointed in himself for having slept through his early morning study time. "Lord, I'm already behind schedule today," he began his impromptu devotions as he straightened his tie and approached the door to the church office. "I slept through my study time again, but it doesn't seem to matter whether I study or not. My sermons are about as motivational as a recorded telephone sales pitch. My visitation is mechanical, committee meetings are disorganized fiascoes, and the other things I do seem fruitless. If my investment in this church was money instead of time, I would have to file for bankruptcy."

Nunson stopped outside the office and stared up at the cloudless sky as if looking for a visible, listening ear. "And even when I do put something together well, these people don't seem to care. Jericho Street Church is aptly named. It's like a walled city, a fortress. Their complacency has shut You out, and they're not letting me in either." The pastor dropped his head and turned to reach for the doorknob. "If You'll show me how to knock these walls down," he sighed with a slight smile, "we can both work from the inside out."

"Happy Tuesday, Pastor," the plump, gray-haired secretary said from her desk as Nunson entered.

"Good morning, Dottie," the pastor was cordial but walked quickly to the solitude of his office.

"Oh, Pastor," Dottie intercepted him. "You already received one call this morning. The Commander wants to see you."

"Commander who?" Nunson stopped abruptly to face her.

"Just, 'The Commander,'" the secretary replied, surprised at her pastor's question. "He said, 'Tell Pastor Nunson that the Commander wants to set up an appointment with him.' I assumed you must know who he was."

"I don't know any Commander," Nunson argued, "and I

don't have time to visit with every old soldier who . . ." For a split second a mysteriously familiar shadow of a military man flashed into Nunson's mind, interrupting his thought. The frighteningly graphic déjà vu sent a tingle up his back as if a squadron of butterflies was loose inside his shirt.

"If he calls again," Nunson resigned, making room for his strange hunch, "tell him I can see him for a few minutes at five this afternoon."

Nunson slid into his Naugahyde swivel chair to collect his thoughts before staff meeting. "The Commander," he snickered, shaking his head at the name. "He's probably some old lifer who needs somebody to listen to his war stories." Scooping up a handful of manila folders, he headed for the conference room.

Pastor Nunson assessed the day's staff meeting to be a depressing waste of time. Each staff member complained about the apathy among the people and the lack of funds to complete church projects. The pastor's drooping attempts to encourage the troops fell short as he battled pangs of personal failure.

The youth pastor added insult to Nunson's depression when he began their private meeting by announcing that he was leaving the church to join the staff of a local campus outreach ministry, "a ministry in this town with a future," the young man added piously.

Nunson stumbled blankly out of his office at 11 A.M. to check his in basket. "The Commander called again," Dottie spoke with an expression of pain on her face and a slight whimper in her voice. It was the same expression and tone, Nunson recalled, that had accompanied her confession to spilling a can of mimeograph ink on the office carpet.

"What's the problem, Dottie?" the pastor pursued.

"The Commander said, 'Tell Pastor Nunson that I'll meet him at the church at five o'clock tomorrow morning.' "

"Five in the morning!" Nunson snapped.

"I'm sorry, Pastor," Dottie lamented. "I never mentioned A.M. or P.M. I just said you could see him at five o'clock. He said, 'Fine, I'll be at the church at 5 A.M. tomorrow,' and hung up."

"Can't you call him back?" Nunson felt indignation steaming around his collar.

"He didn't leave a number or give me any name except 'Commander,'" Dottie whined defensively.

"It's not your fault, Dottie," the pastor consoled. Then he stepped to the window and stared aimlessly above the treetops for several seconds. "And as for you, Commander whoever-you-are," he mumbled to himself, "you can have the entire church to yourself at 5 A.M."

Pastor Nunson's eyelids slid half open to see the fuzzy green symbols 4:55 leering at him from the dresser. "It's that Commander," he grunted with disgust. "I've never even met the kook, and he's waking me up in the middle of the night."

He leaned up on one elbow, pushed the curtains aside, and peeked out toward the empty church parking lot across the street, dimly lit by one fluorescent lamppost. "Just as I thought," he said loudly enough to cause Trina to stir. "The old duffer is a no-show." Then he lowered himself to the pillow and hoped to be asleep soon.

And he would have been, except for the clamor of what Nunson surmised to be the trash truck rumbling down Jericho Street and turning into the church parking lot. "Why can't they put quieter engines on those things or . . ." The pastor's half-asleep plea was short-circuited by a disturbing thought that pushed his eyes fully open. Today is Wednesday. The trash truck comes on Saturday.

The loudly idling engine of an obviously large vehicle outside the window beckoned Nunson to look again, so he did. "Oh my!" he gasped as he jerked out of bed to get a better look. "Oh my!"

Trina complained about the noise without waking, but Nunson didn't hear her. He quickly fumbled his way into his jogging suit, slid into his thongs, and threaded his way through the darkened house to the front door. He wondered whether it was anger, curiosity, or fear that was driving him to investigate the awesome sight that had greeted him out the bedroom window.

The predawn autumn chill pushed Nunson quickly down the porch steps and out to the curb. "Oh my!" he whistled again as the reality of the sight across the street stung him to full consciousness.

The loudly droning engine was that of a huge military troop carrier parked longside the light pole and aimed at the parsonage. Its brilliant high beams shot two misty cones of light to where the pastor stood. About 40 soldiers, Nunson estimated, stood at ease beside the truck. They were dressed in full battle gear with automatic weapons at their sides.

Nunson's mind frantically searched to define what his eyes were receiving: "It's another bad dream. It's a nightmare. It's a Russian invasion. It's . . ."

Suddenly another helmeted soldier marched forward from behind the truck. "Ten-hut!" one soldier barked, and the others instantly clattered to attention. Nunson felt himself stiffen instinctively in the presence of an officer.

The truck's loud engine shut down, but the headlights remained bright behind the strangely familiar silhouette standing on the opposite curb.

"Pastor Nunson," the officer called out, the sound chilling the statue-still clergyman.

"Yes sir," Nunson responded automatically, wishing he hadn't yielded authority to the stranger so quickly.

"I have your orders," the officer called back.

"*You* have *my* orders?" Nunson retorted clearly, anxiety almost audibly crackling in his soul.

"Orders for you and Jericho Street Church," was the Commander's crisp reply.

Nunson summoned all the courage he could find in his rapidly beating heart, pointed a deliberate but respectful finger toward the silhouetted officer and said, "You have invaded my dreams and my thoughts. Now you have awakened me in the middle of the night." The pastor felt fear and confidence battling for supremacy within him, and his whole body began to tremble. "I'm not taking any orders from you until you identify yourself. Now who are you?" Confidence had framed the words, but fear had pushed them out almost as a declaration of war.

The officer spoke immediately: "I am the Commander of the forces of Almighty God."

The words flamed at Nunson like a gigantic ball of blinding light, their inherent truth melting every muscle and tendon in his frame, and he collapsed to the grass by the curb like a marionette whose strings had been abruptly snipped.

"Oh, my dear God!" he prayerfully groaned, sensing panic, fearing death, but powerless to move. "Oh, my dear God! Oh, my dear God!" he sobbed repeatedly.

Pastor Nunson felt as though all his bones were out of joint. His crumpled legs were imprisoned under his large torso, and his arms were draped limply over the top of his head. His face was pressed into the grass and tears flowed profusely into the earth. He expected at any moment to be translated into heaven or executed by the angelic platoon.

When his sobbing had quieted, the Commander was beside him. "I have some instructions for you concerning your work here at Jericho Street Church," the Commander spoke softly. The words flowed into Nunson's spirit like hot coffee into an empty stomach.

The pastor, still unable to move, whispered, "I'm listening, sir."

The Commander leaned closer, and Nunson thought he could hear the rivers of the world rushing in the Commander's breath. "Much work requires much worship." The Commander's instantly familiar words sent torrents of truth gushing into Nunson's heart, as if a dam of insight had burst above a desert of perplexity and discouragement. "You and I can conquer every problem at Jericho Street Church," the Commander continued. "But I only issue battle plans in the throne room."

The curtains of Nunson's mind drew back to reveal a crystal plain supporting a magnificent throne of light seemingly miles from the pastor's vantage point. Surrounding the throne in every direction, loose-jointed and prostrate as he was, Nunson saw pastors and deacons and committees and congregations—millions upon millions of them—worshipfully singing, "Holy, holy, holy, Lord God Almighty."

"Worship before study, worship before preaching," the Commander instructed as Nunson gazed into the heavenly scene, yearning to move closer to the radiant throne.

"Worship before study, worship before preaching," the pastor repeated, his voice still broken.

"Worship before staff meeting, worship before counseling, worship before visitation," the Commander continued and Pastor Nunson echoed. Soon he was on his own: "Holy, holy, holy, Lord God Almighty. Worship before deacons' meeting, worship before committee meetings, worship before church workdays . . ."

By the time Pastor Nunson could lift his head it was about 6 A.M. and the sky was lightening. He was alone on the curb, and the parking lot was empty. It took several more minutes for him to unfold his stiffened limbs, stand to his feet, and hobble slowly to the church.

Upon reaching the altar he resumed his prostrate posture and continued his adoration for another two hours. He repeated the process every succeeding morning for the next three weeks. Then, at Nunson's invitation, deacon chairman Caleb Jefferson joined the pastor at the sunrise altar, followed by the Men's Fellowship president, the church treasurer, and Trina. Each month a few more joined the pastor facedown in what he insisted on calling "The Throne Room." Before too many months had passed the walls of Jericho Street Church fell down flat.

FOR THOUGHT AND DISCUSSION

1. How else could you state the essence of the Commander's message to Pastor Nunson, "Much work requires much worship"?
2. This story is a contemporary recreation of Josh. 5:13-15. According to these verses, why did Joshua prostrate himself? Why did the visitor command Joshua to take off his sandals?
3. What is your definition of worship? How has this story helped you better understand the place of worship in the life of the believer?
4. On a scale of 1 to 10, with 10 being high, how would you rate yourself as a worshiper of God? How might you improve as a worshiper?

10

THE INCIDENT AT CAFFEINE FALLS

"HEY, CAN WE STOP for a rest now?" It was the fifth time chunky, 22-year-old Lanny Binkman had panted for mercy since the hike began. His fellow backpackers—two other singles and one couple from the "Roaring Twenties" Sunday School class, along with their teacher Ralph Cumberland—were also beginning to feel the strain from the arduous ascent of Horse Creek Trail. They finally agreed with Lanny's wheezing demand for a breather.

"OK, troops," Mr. Cumberland called back to where Lanny wobbled under his bulging pack. "We'll take a break as soon as we get into the trees at the top of this ridge." The five youthful hikers shuffled up the steep trail behind their leader, through a patch of jagged, sun-bathed boulders and into the shady cover of a cluster of squatty evergreens.

One by one the young adults trudged into the shade and squirmed out of their packs. Lanny, whose final step barely reached the top of the trail, dumped his pack against the nearest boulder and melted in a heap beside it.

For several moments the hikers sat motionless and panting while buzzing deer flies investigated their sweaty faces. The silent mountain loomed above them on one side, and Horse Creek coursed briskly several hundred feet below them, its muted roar harmonizing with the deer flies' monotone.

Fsst! Lanny had regained just enough strength to open the top flap of his backpack, lift out a can of Pepsi, and pull the tab opener. Mr. Cumberland cocked his head suspiciously from the other end of the short line of reposed hikers. He watched Lanny tip the can to his mouth and suck half its contents down in three huge gulps. "What's that?" asked the tanned and fit 53-year-old teacher.

"It's Pepsi, Mr. Cumberland," Lanny replied, holding the can near his lips with one hand while he stroked it lovingly with the other.

"I can see that it's a can of Pepsi-Cola, Lanny," Ralph was a little irritated, as he most often was when Lanny advanced the blatantly obvious as if it were a new revelation. "What I mean is why is Pepsi-Cola going with us on our backpacking trip into the wild?" Ralph enunciated the words "Pepsi-Cola" with the same tone of disdain that accompanied his use of words like *lust* and *anti-Christ.*

Lanny couldn't answer Ralph's question because he had again tipped the can to his mouth to swig the bottom half of his drink. Loretta Finster and Heidi Wong, the two single girls on the trip, glanced nervously between Lanny and the leader, mirroring the mild tension of confrontation. Shawn and Gina Gibson, who had cut short their honeymoon in order to join their classmates on the trip, were oblivious to everything. They huddled on a decaying log whispering and giggling.

Knowing that she and Heidi would soon be implicated in the Pepsi discussion, Loretta spoke up. "Mr. Cumberland, we know that Pepsi isn't on the list of things you told us to bring on the hike. But this weekend trip is the only vacation some of us will get this summer. And it wouldn't be a vacation without Pepsi."

"We?" Ralph retorted. "Are you telling me that you're *all*

toting cans of Pepsi-Cola into the unspoiled wilderness?"

"Not exactly, sir," Heidi eased into the discussion respectfully. "Lanny is carrying enough Pepsi for the three of us. Loretta and I have the rest of our food in our packs." Lanny couldn't suppress the grin of a bashful hero.

"How much Pepsi-Cola did *we* bring?" Any anger Ralph may have felt about the Pepsi intrusion was absent from his voice. Rather his question was tinged with a disappointed lilt, as if asking his wife why she kept a photograph of Robert Redford on her dressing table.

"We were able to stuff 24 cans and some dry ice into Lanny's pack," Loretta answered proudly.

"But it's only 10:30 in the morning," Ralph protested weakly, still uncomfortable at the thought of such rank commercialization of his beloved outdoors. "Isn't it a little early for soda?"

"I have one or two cans every morning at the bus stop on my way to work," Heidi boasted.

"I always get a Big Gulp at Seven-Eleven during my morning coffee break and sip on it till lunchtime," Loretta added.

"And you haven't lived—" Lanny paused to savor the thought—"until you've had a bowl of Froot Loops for breakfast with Pepsi poured over them." Ralph dropped his face into his hands attempting to hide an involuntary wince of disgust that he knew was squeezing the Christianity out of his countenance.

"Speaking of morning coffee break," Loretta continued, hoping that Ralph was at least resigned to their disclosure, "how about passing me a cold one, Lanny." Heidi added a lip-licking "Amen" to Loretta's suggestion. The Gibsons were still cooing on the log, and Ralph excused himself with a sigh.

Lanny struggled to his feet to dig into his pack while the two girls reclined against their packs to await, with mouths watering, Lanny's service. He pulled one of the coldest cans from its bed of dry ice, snapped open the tab, and stepped toward Loretta. But his large army boot snagged a shoulder strap, and his first stride jerked the top-heavy backpack to the trail with a crash. Lanny lost his balance and belly-flopped into the dirt with an "oof." Loretta's can of Pepsi tumbled from Lanny's hand on impact, and its contents fizzed out into the soil.

"Our Pepsi!" Loretta and Heidi screamed in unison as they jumped to their feet. Their terror-filled outburst snapped Shawn and Gina out of their trance and sent a curious squirrel scampering back up a tree.

"It's OK, girls," Lanny began with a groan, prostrate at their feet. "I'll get you another . . ." Lanny looked up to see the girls pointing wildly down the trail. Their fingers were aimed at a disorganized parade of shiny red, white, and blue cans bouncing rapidly down the steep trail the troupe had just ascended. The brightly colored cans were followed by several chunks of dry ice, a stick of deodorant, a can of shaving cream, and a roll of toilet tissue. Gravity was summoning the contents of Lanny's dumped pack to the brink of the trailside cliff and an unbroken fall to the creek below.

The three hikers scrambled frantically down the trail trying to catch the platoon of cans bounding helplessly toward the precipice. But the Pepsi had an unquenchable lead. Lanny, Loretta, and Heidi skidded to an abrupt halt at the cliff's edge in time to see the last can plunge over the side with an unfurled, fluttering ribbon of floral print tissue as an escort. The sound of the cans smashing into the rocks below was swallowed by Horse Creek's overpowering roar.

"Oh, no!" Lanny whimpered breathlessly as if he had just failed in an attempt to rescue a drowning friend.

"Way to go, klutz foot," Heidi snarled in Lanny's direction as she and Loretta surveyed the gleaming wreckage at the base of the cliff. Shawn and Gina, arms locked together, were still inching down to the cliff's edge when Ralph Cumberland streaked by them, fearful that his largest and most inept student had done himself in. But the supply-strewn trail from the upended pack to the cliff told the true story.

Ralph stopped beside his students and stared silently over the edge at the Pepsi on the rocks.

"The trail ahead of us winds down to the creek bank in a couple of miles," Ralph informed, more concerned about the litter beside the creek than the loss of over two gallons of soft drinks. "We'll make camp there and hike back upstream this afternoon to clean up the debris."

Ralph and the Gibsons headed back up the trail while Lanny apologized weakly to Loretta and Heidi for his clumsiness. His two friends grunted their forgiveness. They trudged somberly back to their packs, retrieving Lanny's surviving toiletries as they went. Loretta's unsipped can of Pepsi was smashed in the dirt where it had been trampled in the rescue attempt. Lanny stuffed the flattened aluminum can into his pack.

"I wouldn't worry about losing all that soda," Ralph consoled as they all struggled into their packs. He was sorry about his students' disappointment but secretly glad the Pepsi had made good its escape. "We're in the woods now. You don't need all that artificial color and flavor. Besides, that stuff is loaded with caffeine. It's really not good for you."

"I hate to tell you this, Mr. Cumberland," Lanny interrupted his teacher's moralizing. "But my Old Spice, T.P., and our Pepsis weren't the only items that went over the side." Ralph stopped cinching his waist strap and glared at Lanny questioningly. "Remember the jar of instant coffee you asked me to carry for you?"

"Not my coffee!" the leader shrieked. Again he covered his face with his hands.

"We're in the woods now, Mr. Cumberland," Lanny mimicked, winking at Loretta and Heidi. "That stuff is loaded with caffeine. It's really not good for you." Ralph Cumberland was cornered and he knew it. He sheepishly joined his students in a good laugh.

By early afternoon the hikers had wound down the trail to their proposed campsite alongside the creek. After eating lunch and setting up camp, the group headed upstream with fishing poles in hand to find the crash site. After a slow trek over rocks and fallen logs they arrived at the location Lanny had dubbed Caffeine Falls. The shattered cans of Pepsi resembled exploded bomb casings, and the jar of Folgers instant crystals was smashed to smithereens in a small pool that was colored dark brown.

Having stuffed the collected trash into Ralph's knapsack, the group set out for camp, casting their fishing lines into every shadowy pool along the way. When several of their bites got away, Lanny theorized that the energetic fish in the creek were probably on a sugar high from the Pepsi in the creek. Horse Creek Canyon echoed with riotous laughter.

It was nearly nine o'clock by the time dinner was over. The forest night was accompanied by a stinging high altitude chill, and the hikers clustered together around their glowing fire pit. With their stomachs filled with trout and their fingers sticky with melted marshmallows, the tired travelers sang a few nonsensical campfire songs and laughed together about the incident at Caffeine Falls and their frantic attempt to save the backsliding cans of Pepsi-Cola.

"I sure wish I had a can of Pepsi right now," Lanny fantasized aloud, his tongue licking his lips between two chubby cheeks.

"Me too!" Heidi chimed in. The three young adults debated in wide-eyed detail the merits of *real* Pepsi—not the caffeine-free or diet kind—and the tingly-burny sensation an ice-cold gulp brought to the gullet.

"I can't remember a day when I didn't drink at least one Pepsi," Loretta was almost moaning. "This is a national tragedy."

Ralph stirred the coals gently and added another small log. "I must admit that it's been a long time since I've gone without coffee too," he confessed. "It doesn't seem like camping without a cup of 'mud' in my hands."

The weary campers stared blankly at the flaming logs evolving to red-orange coals. They sang a few love songs to Jesus and felt very close to Him and to each other. Ralph quietly realized a new appreciation for Lanny, Loretta, and Heidi as he evaluated the day's events and minor conflicts. The teacher closed their first day of hiking with a quiet prayer, and they all slipped into sleeping bags.

Ralph Cumberland and his three single students were anything but chatterboxes as they arose, built a fire, and started breakfast. Ralph mechanically set a pot of water on to boil for coffee before he remembered that instant Folgers had been unceremoniously dropped from the menu along with Pepsi-Cola. Several times he caught himself looking around for his missing mug of coffee and scowled disapprovingly each time.

Lanny, Loretta, and Heidi were a little off center too. They absentmindedly surveyed the campsite as if looking for cans of Pepsi that had been left for them like manna during the night. At some point in their first waking hours each of the four muttered something like, "I don't know how I'm going to function without my customary liquid kick-start."

After breakfast the group broke camp and continued their trek along Horse Creek Trail. Loretta took the lead for the first mile, hoping with every bend in the trail to find a Seven-Eleven where she would gladly trade everything in her pack—except her cosmetic case—for a Big Gulp. Heidi was mentally inventorying her equipment to determine what she would offer a stranger on the trail in exchange for cans of Pepsi he might be carrying. And Lanny, whose craving for Pepsi was still a few hours behind his friends' early signs of withdrawal, was thinking ahead. If we keep hiking instead of making camp tonight, he plotted to himself, we can reach the main highway by midnight and ambush a passing Pepsi truck.

Ralph Cumberland followed the three singles on the trail. He was quoting Bible verses to himself, trying to keep his mind off a severe case of the coffeeless jitters. The Gibsons brought up the rear. Besides Horse Creek's persistent, babbling *whish,* the only sound on the trail was from Shawn—a biology major in college—and his bride. He described the flora and fauna along the trail in scientific terms, and Gina giggled her approval.

The hikers slid out of their packs at noon near a bend in the creek that rushed white and clean over a valley of rocks. "Does anybody have an aspirin?" Loretta begged, mopping her forehead with a bandanna she had soaked in the cold stream. "I have a headache."

"That's funny, so do I," Heidi said as she scooped her Sierra cup full of water from the creek. "Was it something we ate?"

"It's partly from the altitude, but it is aggravated by a withdrawal from caffeine since the incident at Caffeine Falls yesterday," Ralph was rubbing his own forehead empathetically.

"Withdrawal?" Lanny quizzed between mouthfuls of trail mix. His head was just beginning to tingle with discomfort.

"That's right," Shawn interjected authoritatively. "Caffeine is a mild but addictive stimulant found in coffee, tea, many soft drinks, chocolate, and some medicines." Gina giggled again at her husband's knowledge.

Shawn proceeded to remind the group that he and Gina did not partake of Pepsi, coffee, or any substances that might endanger the health of their future children. Gina blushed and blinked her agreement. Ralph silently determined that some day Shawn would probably be the surgeon general of the United States.

"That makes me think of a verse we read in Sunday School a few months ago," Loretta was unwrapping a raspberry fruit roll as she spoke. "It went something like, 'Everything is OK for me, but I will not let myself become controlled by anything.' "

"That verse is in 1 Corinthians 6," Ralph was encouraged by Loretta's recall. He recognized the emergence of a teachable moment but also realized that he was one of the students. "Tell us what you are thinking, Loretta."

The group leaned slightly closer together in order to hear Loretta clearly above the endlessly chattering creek. "When we studied that verse in class I applied it to alcohol and drugs—stuff I dabbled in before I became a Christian. I know about the caffeine buzz Shawn is talking about, but I guess I never saw Pepsi in the same category of substances that can control me."

She paused and squinted as a dozen racquetballs ricocheted painfully off the inner walls of her skull. She framed her next words carefully because she knew they would implicate two of her best friends and her Sunday School teacher. "Maybe God allowed us to experience the incident at Caffeine Falls yesterday to reveal something that is wrongfully mastering us." Horse Creek continued to babble noisily, but the hikers lapsed into thoughtful silence.

"God has been talking to me about my coffee habit ever since that lesson," Ralph confessed with a deep sigh. "And I think you're right, Loretta. We have a perfect opportunity here to break away from a subtle but demanding master." Heidi and Lanny hummed affirmatively.

Ralph reached into the side pocket of his pack and pulled out a small bottle of aspirin. "These tablets will relieve our headaches," he announced as he displayed the bottle, "but they contain caffeine, too, and may only suspend our addiction. If we forego the aspirin, our headaches should be gone by morning and we'll be off caffeine altogether. What do you say?"

"Let's dump the caffeine cold turkey!" Loretta urged.

"We'll be completely decaffeinated!" Heidi agreed hopefully. Lanny was not as enthusiastic, but he agreed. Ralph returned the aspirin bottle to his pack unopened. The Gibsons applauded the brave pioneers enthusiastically.

As they packed their lunch supplies the campers agreed that neither Pepsi, coffee, nor aspirin were wrong in themselves. It was the mastery of these substances and others over Christians that was at cross-purposes with the Bible's teaching. They also voiced their need to remain supportive and accountable to one another when they returned home to abundant supplies of Pepsi and Folgers.

After a few hundred feet on the trail, Lanny had composed new words to a familiar hiking tune that all six of them recalled from their youth. Under Lanny's raucous direction, the sextet launched into a lusty concert on the trail, which was to be long remembered as their backpacking theme song:

Ninety-nine cans of caffeine on the trail,
Ninety-nine cans of caffeine;
Roll them all over Caffeine Falls,
Ninety-eight cans of caffeine on the trail.

FOR THOUGHT AND DISCUSSION

1. Spiritually speaking, would you put Lanny, Loretta, Heidi, and Ralph Cumberland in the same category as more serious substance abusers (marijuana, cocaine, pills, etc.)? Why or why not?
2. Read 1 Cor. 6:19-20. How many reasons can you find in these verses for a Christian's conscientious approach to any ingested substance?
3. What are some other ways Christians are involved in subtle substance abuse?
4. Are there any foods, liquids, or other substances to which you are psychologically or habitually addicted? What steps do you need to take to free yourself from unnecessary substance abuse?

11

THE FILLING STATIONS OF KIRKSBURG

IT SO HAPPENED that all four filling stations in the community of Kirksburg were located on the four corners of First and Main.

United Refinery, the oldest station in town, was on the northeast corner. United's patrons were mostly retirees who had their cars serviced regularly even though they traveled only a few miles each week. The attendants at United were all deeply involved in community service projects in Kirksburg.

On the northwest corner stood First Gas, a franchise station of a national oil company. First Gas had built a loyal clientele by maintaining a clean, efficient, token-operated car wash. Customers were given a free wash with every fill-up.

Community Oil, on the southwest corner, was part of a chain of loosely affiliated independents that believed in spending money to make money. Community boasted computerized pumps and the latest in diagnostic equipment for auto repair. Community's mechanic was factory trained and knew practically everything there was to know about fixing cars.

On the southeast corner of the intersection was Fuel Center, the only 24-hour station in Kirksburg. Fuel Center sported two shiny tow trucks and offered round-the-clock emergency road service and towing. Fuel Center's pump jockeys were always ready to serve motorists in trouble.

It was the custom of the four station owners to meet at nearby Angelo's Diner for lunch once each month. The men usually avoided talking about their respective successes and problems due to a natural sense of healthy competition. But one particular day a wave of courageous abandon swept the conversation beyond its usual limits.

"It's the car wash that's keeping us alive," confided the owner of First Gas. "It's chicken feed to maintain, but it brings in the customers for fill-ups and attracts a lot of drivers who just want a free car wash."

"Reliable auto repairs—that's what keeps customers coming back," advanced the Community Oil man. "We dropped a bundle into all that equipment, and our mechanic pulls down a handsome hourly wage. But the people who come in for repairs usually come back for gas, tires, and windshield wipers."

"You probably don't realize how many people we attract with our 24-hour road service," bragged Fuel Center's owner. "People want the security of knowing that someone is available to help them when they're in trouble."

"Community involvement shows people you care," spoke the head of United Refinery. "Each one of my men has won a host of customers through his tireless efforts to improve the community of Kirksburg."

The four men sat in thoughtful silence for several minutes as a worm of greed wriggled through their minds. Then each excused himself and hurried off toward his own corner of First and Main, leaving Angelo with four plates of delicious pasta that were barely touched.

All during the next month the intersection vibrated with noisy activity: jackhammers, bulldozers, construction crews. When the dust settled, all three rivals of First Gas proclaimed the grand opening of newly installed car washes. The three stations opposite Community Oil hoisted banners declaring, "Mechanic on Duty." A husky new tow truck sat proudly in each of the stations facing Fuel Center, and signs in all four windows announced 24-hour service. And the monthly lunch meeting at Angelo's was postponed indefinitely because each owner, following United Refinery's lead, was hobnobbing at noon with the Kiwanis, Lions, Optimists, or Elks.

The fight was on. Banners blared from all four stations: "Free Car Wash with Fill-up." Four giant ads in the Kirksburg Bulletin clamored for the town's auto repair dollars. And the local radio station jingled the virtues of each station's emergency road service.

For almost two months the corner of First and Main was jammed with traffic night and day as motorists from three counties swarmed into Kirksburg like kids to a carnival. But soon the banners began to fade, the newspaper ads became commonplace, and the incessant radio jingles began to jangle the nerves of the population. Gasoline prices at all four stations began to spiral upward while profits nosedived as the four stations frantically tried to outbid each other for customers. Soon First and Main took on the appearance of the county fairgrounds the week after the fair closed.

On one especially quiet morning, Angelo stepped out of his diner and bellowed into the silent intersection, "Hey, gas men, the coffee is on the house!" All four owners walked silently into the diner and eased into their familiar corner booth. Heads were down, and no one spoke.

"Hey, gas men," Angelo broke the silence as he clunked four mugs of steaming coffee on the table, "let me ask you a question." Each man collected a mug and looked soberly into Angelo's round face. "If I wanted the best steak dinner in town, where should I go?"

The four men glanced curiously at each other, then looked up at big Angelo who stood over them. "The Beef House on Fourteenth Street," one of them answered matter-of-factly. The others nodded, but they all wondered why Angelo asked such a strange question.

"And what about Chinese food? Who makes the best?" Angelo pursued.

"The Jade Garden," the men around the table chimed in unison.

"And pasta?" Angelo beamed. "Where's the best?"

"Right here, Angelo. You make the best pasta in the state. But what are you driving at?"

Angelo placed his two fat hands in the middle of the table and leaned into the quartet of gas men like a quarterback about to call a play. "When somebody walks in here and orders a steak, I say, 'You want a good steak? Go over to the Beef House. They grill the best steaks in town.' And if somebody has their taste buds set for Chinese food, I send them to the Jade Garden because nobody can make sweet and sour pork like Chin Ling.

"But when somebody comes here for linguine," Angelo's face beamed proudly, "I say, 'You've come to the right place. My linguine will teach your mouth to sing in Italian!' " The gas men even chuckled a little at Angelo's description. "It seems that we in the Kirksburg restaurant business have learned well what my mother used to tell us kids: 'Find out what you do good, and then do it the best.' "

Suddenly the four pairs of eyes around the table gleamed with insight. "Say, Angelo," spoke up one enlightened gas station owner. "Where would you go in Kirksburg for a quality car wash?"

Angelo rose to his full stature again. "First Gas," he answered quickly. "They have the best car wash unit in the county."

"How about a tune-up?" asked another.

"No contest," again Angelo answered without hesitation. "Community Oil's mechanic has hands like a surgeon."

"Emergency road service?" asked another.

"Fuel Center has two tough trucks, and those guys

know how to get you on the road fast," Angelo answered with authority. "And when you want to know what's what in Kirksburg, the guys at United Refinery have the low-down."

About a month later a 16-foot rent-a-truck with out-of-state plates swayed heavily into Fuel Center and stopped at the pump.

"Can I help you?" greeted the attendant warmly as he approached a man stepping out of the cab.

"Hi," the driver answered as he stretched almost a hundred miles out of his weary back. "We're just moving into town and we're gonna need a gas station to care for our car."

The attendant nodded. "We're all good at keeping your tank full of gas, tires full of air, and radiator full of coolant," he said as he motioned toward the other three filling stations. "But when you need repairs, call Community Oil. They're the best, and we send everybody there. First Gas has a top flight car wash system, and United can tell you what's going on in town. And if you ever need gas in the middle of the night or you're stuck out on the highway, you can call on us."

"Great!" the newcomer exclaimed. "What a thoughtful, efficient approach to community car care. Now, what about the churches in town?"

The attendant grinned. "Maybe you better ask Angelo," he chuckled, jerking a thumb toward the diner. "He's recently been chosen to host the monthly meeting of the Kirksburg Ministerial Association."

FOR THOUGHT AND DISCUSSION

1. What do you think the filling stations and their specialties represent in this allegory?
2. Read 1 Cor. 12:21-26. What attitudes among churches tend to disrupt Christian unity in a community? What is the proper attitude churches should hold toward each other?
3. Who ought to be playing the role of Angelo in bringing churches together in a community?
4. What can you do to effect a positive atmosphere and actions among the churches in your area?

12

ADAMWAITS

IT WAS BARELY DAYLIGHT, but Josiah was already loading the last of his few supplies onto his lean horse Baldy. The animal shifted nervously, expectantly, as Josiah cinched his bedroll behind the saddle. The air was stiff with an icy, autumn-morning chill. Josiah jerked his coat collar around his ears and added an extra wool shirt, some corn, and a few hunks of dried beef to his leather satchel.

This oughta be enough, he said to himself, anticipating only a two-day trip from the mountain farm to Black Bear. Baldy swung his head around and breathed a puff of steam. Josiah slapped a large hand to his rump. Returning the lantern to the barn he saw the figure of a young boy plodding toward him.

"You gonna go now, Josiah?" Adam asked, wiping the sleep from his eyes.

"I reckon it's time, Bub. I was just comin' to get you out of bed." Josiah's parents had adopted Adam as a baby after his parents were killed in an Indian massacre. The two strolled toward the barn, Adam scuffling along in a pair of Josiah's old boots. Josiah swung his arm around his brother's shoulders.

"With Pa gone," he explained, "this isn't the place for us, Bub. You need schoolin' and that means city livin'. I'm gonna find somebody in Black Bear to buy our stock."

"Can't I go with you?" Adam tried not to whine. Josiah gently poked a finger in the boy's ribs. Adam let out a playful squeal.

"Somebody's gotta keep an eye on the stock while I'm gone or there won't be nuthin' to sell when I get back." Adam understood. Cougars prey on defenseless, unguarded animals. Someone did have to stay behind.

When they reached the barn, Josiah snuffed out the lantern. The gray light of morning penetrated the trees, illuminating the farmyard. Three large sheepdogs excitedly raced among the cornstalks beyond the barn to inspect some small intruder. The brothers walked slowly back to the readied horse.

"Pa would be proud of you, Bub," Josiah said as he mounted. "You're a real man now." He paused to put on his gloves, then smiled. "I don't know how long I'll be gone, but I *will* be back. Remember that." He reached down and shook Adam gently on the back of the neck.

Baldy set off at a canter across the meadow to the fence. When Josiah reached the gate, he turned and yelled, "You keep watchin' for me, Bub. I'll be back as soon as I can." Adam waved until Josiah disappeared between the rows of pines that led down the mountainside.

Throughout the day, Adam followed his brother in his thoughts. They had taken that trip together several times. Adam could imagine Josiah passing every familiar landmark.

At noon, Adam sat with his dogs in the doorway of the barn devouring biscuits and dried beef. He knew Josiah would be crossing the river for the first time about then. The sky was clear and warm. He could picture his brother and Baldy taking a long drink from the crystal spring. How he longed to be there with him.

Later that afternoon, while riding his own horse from the spring, Adam figured his brother would be emerging from the forest onto the rock bed. His father once explained that a rock slide had literally buried that area. He oughta be crossin' the stream again and makin' camp for the night, Adam thought, feeling more lonely than ever.

The next day, Adam circled his horse behind the farmhouse and the cornfield to the west end of the meadow. A hand-hewn rail fence bordered the generous grazing land. He stopped at a place he had visited many times; he looped his horse's reins over a well-worn portion of the railing.

At the base of a long grassy slope were two markers. One was a weathered pine plank with an inscription neatly and delicately carved: EVA COURTNEY 1809-1851. The other was fresh and obviously carved by a younger hand: FARRELL COURTNEY 1811-1858. Adam stood for several moments. He missed his parents terribly, but there was always Josiah.

Suddenly, a flash of terror shot through his veins. His mind fastened on a concept of aloneness he had never known before. What would happen to me if Josiah didn't come back? he thought. He visualized his adopted mother being swept to her death in a raging river. The scene had only been described to him, but he could relive every detail. And now his father was gone. Pa's stomach pains had begun Friday afternoon three weeks ago and by Saturday night he was dead.

Adam stood unmoving, barely breathing, not wanting to carry his thoughts further. He pulled himself onto his horse's back and quickly galloped across the meadow to start the cattle toward the corral.

On the third night, the dogs drove a cougar away with their hysterical barking. Adam thought of Josiah continually. He could suppress the deep fear that had nearly overwhelmed him yesterday, but his mind repeatedly suggested threats of stalking tragedy. The terror grew cancerously in Adam's mind as dark mysteries grow when night falls on the mountains. He comforted himself with the confidence: "I know he'll come back. He said he's coming back."

On the seventh day, Adam hurt himself. He had hiked

down to the stream for water just before evening. The dogs were skipping back and forth lapping at the bubbles swirling behind the rocks. On the far side of the stream, he tried to return to the opposite bank with a wooden bucket full of water. He lost his balance and fell, scraping his calf. The dogs pranced by him unsympathetically as he limped to the farmhouse with a half-full bucket.

During the night, the pain throbbing in his leg wakened him. For the first time since his brother left, Adam cried. The loneliness, fear, and pain made him sob out loud, "Please come back, Josiah, please." Then he slept soundly until morning.

Despite his growing fear, Adam busied himself with morning chores. He didn't even notice Cleon and Billy until their horses had brought them halfway across the meadow. "Hey, Adam," Billy hollered. Cleon and his son, Billy, owned the hardware store in Black Bear. They were taking in the last hunt before winter. Adam anxiously waited for news from Josiah.

The older man talked and talked. Then he reached into his leather coat and handed Adam a neatly folded piece of paper. The pair wished Adam well, turned and galloped toward the mountain trail.

"Dear Bub," the note began. "All is fine down here. I should be home in a few days with Mr. Silva who wants to see our stock. Keep up the chores. Josiah Courtney."

Adam's heart almost burst with joy. He grinned several times throughout the day as he fingered the folded note in his shirt pocket. He was convinced now, and his fears began to fade. He called for his dogs, and the troop chased chickens in playful, squawking, feather-filled confusion.

Adam took on projects of love for Josiah. With an oversized hammer he fixed the loose and fallen boards on the barn. The next morning he hacked away tall grass around the house, barely missing the flowers his father had planted that spring. He forgot all about the abrasion on his leg. His days hummed with activity.

On the 12th night the cougar returned. Adam woke in a cold sweat as the dogs sounded their frantic warning. He hid under his quilt hoping the intruder would go away; but the frenzied yipping continued. Slipping out of bed, he pulled on his pants and boots and grabbed his rifle from the fireplace mantel. The frozen air pressed his head and bare arms. He crossed the yard and saw the dogs barking wildly in the direction of the west meadow.

He barely made out the form of an animal standing next to the fence 40 feet from his parents' grave site. The boy bit his lip in expectation and slipped his finger around the trigger. The cougar seemed to hesitate before it suddenly bounded over the railing and disappeared into the black pines. Almost immediately the dogs quieted. Adam sighed heavily.

As he walked back to the house, a thought occurred to him: I wasn't afraid. I was as strong as Josiah. He returned the gun to the mantel, added two logs to the fire, and climbed back into bed.

Two days later Adam decided to circle the farm and inspect the fences. He had seen his father do it many times. After milking the cows and turning them loose to pasture, he set about his lengthy tour. His father used to ride along the fence and frequently kick the rails for possible weaknesses. But Adam couldn't reach the railing from his high mount. He had to settle for a visual inspection.

He paused at a well-known spot where the rail was worn smooth. "I'm so glad you left Josiah for me," Adam said toward his parents' graves. "He'll watch after me just like you did."

Rapid barking interrupted Adam's thoughts. He whirled his horse around to search for danger. Two horsemen were riding through the gate approaching the house. It was Josiah and Mr. Silva.

"Pack your things, Bub!" Josiah shouted. Adam's heart jumped. "We're movin'!"

FOR THOUGHT AND DISCUSSION

1. This story allegorizes the hope of Christ's return. With this in mind, what do the following elements represent: Josiah? Adam? Josiah's trip? Adam's chores? The cougar?
2. Read Acts 1:10-11. Based on these verses and others you may remember on this theme, what do we know about Christ's return?
3. What is the Christian's task(s) while waiting for Christ's return?
4. What is your greatest concern in the light of the imminent return of Jesus Christ?